The Devil in Disguise

The Devil in Disguise

Ginnie Hole

Firefly Books

SBN 904724 03 4

First published in 1975 by
Firefly Books Limited
49 Lansdowne Place, Hove, Sussex
Made and printed in Great Britain by
The Garden City Press Limited
Letchworth, Hertfordshire SG6 1JS

Contents

Introduction

IT HAPPENED on the train between Greenwich and Charing Cross. I was reading a book about the Devil.

"What is that book?"

I looked up when I heard the question, and saw a small, bespectacled lady in a red headscarf, staring at me reproachfully. I gave a sort of half polite smile and held the book out to show her. To my astonishment and dismay, she grabbed it and began turning over the pages. Then she shut the book firmly and tucked it under her arm.

"You must not read this. It is very dangerous. The Devil —he can take hold of you. You may never be able to rid yourself of him."

Although I have long believed in the Devil as a symbol, as a sort of portrait of evil (by which I mean things like cruelty, war, disease, hate, hunger and pain), I did not believe in such a personal enemy Devil as she was talking about. I tried, unsuccessfully, not to grin.

"Unless you promise never to open this book again, I will not let you have it."

My grin disappeared. The book belonged to the Kensington Public Library.

"You can't do that," I said.

The small lady got up. We were coming into Waterloo—her stop, it seemed. My (or rather the library's) book was still tucked underneath her arm.

"All right," I said, "I won't read it any more."

The small lady looked at me suspiciously. "You promise?"

"Yes," I replied convincingly. She returned the book and got off the train.

As soon as she was out of sight, I opened the book and started reading again—but a bit uneasily. Is telling lies the Devil's work? I wondered. And that was not all; for some time afterwards I almost felt a sinister presence close by, watching me . . .

The stories in this book do not have a lot to do with solid facts. They are all based on legends, or on real historical events that have been so embroidered by the imaginations of the people who talked about them that they are near to becoming legends.

The stories all come from Western Europe. The Devil who appears in them is therefore the Devil of the Christian Faith.

"And there was war in heaven: Michael and his angels fought against the dragon; and the dragon fought and his angels,

"And prevailed not; neither was their place found any more in heaven.

"And the great dragon was cast out, that old serpent, called the Devil, and Satan, which deceiveth the whole world: he was cast out into the earth, and his angels were cast out with him." Revelations 12.

This Devil, whether he be called Satan or Lucifer or Old Nick, has, as his main purpose, to fight God and destroy Christianity. He goes to tremendous trouble, using every kind of temptation and cunning to corrupt people—including a remarkable range of disguises.

The Devil of the Christians is, however, less powerful than the God of the Christians, provided that man gives God the smallest chance. If man is wicked enough or foolish enough to ignore God's offers of help, he is bound to suffer. Only a minority manages to sin and get away with it. That is the thinking that lies at the bottom of most of these stories.

The stories span a period of ten centuries—from the time of Charlemagne's Saxon wars in the eighth century to the last witch trials in eighteenth-century Britain. Throughout this time, Christianity was a far more powerful force than it is now; especially in the middle ages, when most of the legends—from Faustus to Jack o' Kentchurch—began. The story of the monk and his sculpture (also medieval) is very unusual in its outcome of triumph for sin.

It is not always easy to pin down when and where a legend began. In this book, it is only really possible in the case of "The Devil's Cats" and "The Headless Bear", the two stories in which the element of history is greater than that of legend. Margaret Nin-Gilbert, we know, died in Caithness in 1719. Stephen and his wife lived in Ditcheat, Somerset, in the mid-seventeenth century.

Many legends, like "The Rings that Burned" (I used a Breton version), appear in slightly different forms in different parts of Europe. The story of "The Victim" probably comes from Scandinavia, but it found new life in eighteenth-century Germany, when a man named Georg Schmidt was tried for sorcery and charged with casting enchanted bullets.

We do not know exactly when people started telling the legend of St Dunstan and his temptress; however, we do know that it must have been after the tenth century, when Dunstan lived. Different places claim the legend. The version in this book takes place at Glastonbury; but another version is told at Mayfield, about twelve miles from Tunbridge Wells, in which the Devil is said to have cooled his nose in the waters of the wells and given them their iron flavour.

Jack, in "Old Nick", lived, we know, in Kentchurch, Herefordshire. The theories about who he actually was range from Owen Glendower in hiding to a vicar of Kentchurch. Although the character belongs to a particular place, elements in the stories about him are told in slightly different form in other parts of Europe about quite other characters who encounter the Devil. Compare, for example, the ending of this story with the ending of "A Dangerous Bargain". At the same time, there is in the small area surrounding Kentchurch a quite different version of Jack's story, in which he did sell his soul to the Devil, who was to keep it whether he was buried inside the church or out of it. Jack had himself buried in the church wall, foiling the Devil again.

Between the tricks people play on him, the priests that exorcise him, the dogs that oppose him, all with God on their side, the Devil rarely seems to come out on top over those ten centuries. I can't help feeling a little sorry for him. He can be silly, malevolent, attractive and tempting, or spine-chilling. But in all these guises he seems to work extremely hard for what turns out to be very small success. But I can't say I wish him better luck in the future.

I

Black Simon

"SIMON! HERE, lad!"

John's voice sounded unexpectedly loud in the dark forest. Every living thing apart from himself and his two dogs had vanished, frightened by the storm that had been raging most of the day. He wished he'd been able to shelter like the forest animals. He felt exhausted, sodden and lonely.

Above the dull beating of the raindrops John heard a slight cracking of twigs and a swish of wet leaves. A huge dark shape loomed at the edge of the clearing. A moment later Black Simon was once again at his heel. John patted the dog's damp muzzle; it was comforting to have him by his side.

His second dog, Patch, was huddled beneath a tall tree at the edge of the clearing. The two dogs looked very alike, big, black sturdy creatures with laughing expressions. Strangers could only tell them apart because Patch had a white mark on her chest. Simon appeared to be completely black, though John knew that he had four white hairs at the base of his throat—to keep the Devil from harming him, the village people would say. John had no time for such fairy tales. For him there was a far more important difference between the dogs. Patch was a good and faithful servant. Black Simon was a friend.

John was head gamekeeper of Diebedale forest in the Highlands of Scotland. He had been out since dawn checking that no deer had come to any harm in the storm, making sure that their shelters were secure and that they had plenty of fodder.

It was now nearly midnight. The rain had not let up once. It had found its way through his oilskins and into his boots. His teeth were chattering; his dogs too were shaking with cold. He longed for the good things in life—food and drink, company, cheerful music, a dance perhaps with bagpipes playing, a pretty girl, a fire with the dogs lying contentedly beside it, and, above all, sleep.

"Let's sleep," he muttered to Black Simon.

The dog took no notice, but ran across to the path that led back towards their home.

"No, boy! We'll stay here for the night. The storm's over. We can shelter from the rain like the forest animals. Like Patch," he added, glancing at the other dog, who was lying down now beneath the tall tree.

Black Simon growled. John knew that he did not like his plan, but he was too tired to care. He sat down beside Patch. Sleep surrounded him like a huge soft blanket. He let his head sink down on to the dog's wet flank and fell asleep.

CRASH!

A terrible sound tore at his eardrums. The clearing was bright as day. Black Simon was rushing at him, snarling. No! This couldn't be real! Simon would never attack him!

He felt a sharp pain in his forearm: Simon's teeth. The dog was tugging at his sleeve, trying to pull him to his feet.

"Back, boy! Back!" he yelled.

Black Simon took no notice. John felt wide awake now. Simon's mad, he thought. The storm has sent him mad. John scrambled to his feet. The dog was powerful enough to kill him now that he had turned against him.

Black Simon jerked him violently across the clearing, which was, at that same moment, bathed in light again.

CRACK! The tall tree under which John had been sheltering trembled, burst into flames, and fell like a guillotine on the very spot where he had just been sleeping. John felt sick. He was shaking all over. It was as if he had witnessed his own death.

Black Simon was already walking along the homeward path, followed closely by Patch. He saved my life, thought John. How did he know the tree was about to be struck by lightning? John looked searchingly at Simon, so calm and gentle now. Perhaps he understood more than John did. Then he laughed at himself. He was being just like the village people, imagining all sorts of silly things. He caught up with the dogs. The storm was definitely over now. Even the rain had stopped at last. There was a bright moon. The horror of the last few minutes was slowly lifting.

"Thanks, Simon lad," he murmured, stroking the dog's head.

As he did so Simon came to an abrupt halt. John felt his ears go rigid. He knew the dog had heard something. Patch too was standing with ears pricked, listening. Then John, with his inferior human ears, began to hear . . . a faint, keen note: Music! It grew louder and stronger. He recognized the instrument now; it was the bagpipes he knew and loved so well. But this music wasn't merely joyful. It was thrilling. It seemed to promise him the world.

"Simon! Patch!" John turned in the direction the music was coming from. There was no need to follow the path. They could go home a different way, through the trees and past the Poacher's Pool. Towards the music. John hurried forward eagerly, dizzily, almost running.

He glanced round to check that his dogs were at his heels. They weren't there. They were still standing on the path.

"Come on!" he roared angrily.

The dogs did not move. Never mind; they could find their own way home. John did not stop to wonder whether he could find his way, although this was the part of the forest he knew least well.

He usually steered clear of the Poacher's Pool. It had got its name because many years ago a well-known poacher had been found at the bottom of it, dead. All over his body there had been curious purple-red marks, like scorch-marks, for which nobody could find an explanation; except the village people, who said that the marks had been made by the Devil. John didn't believe that rubbish. But he avoided the pool, all the same.

Above the music there came a faint howl. John looked back at his dogs again. He had left them far behind. The music seemed to come nearer. It drowned the howl. A cloud covered the moon. The dogs were hidden in the blackness of the night. Only the music mattered now.

For a moment John wondered how he would be able to go on without a light. Then he realized that it was not as dark as he had thought. Ahead of him was an orange glow, as if given off by the embers of a fire, promising warmth and comfort after the long, cold day. As he got nearer he saw that it was coming from a house. From that same house came the music.

John was puzzled by the house. Surely he would have known about it, unless it was new. But it did not look new. Its solid stone walls were so overgrown with mosses that it appeared green; it glistened with a soft underwater sheen that contrasted oddly with the bright orange squares of its windows. It must have been here for years to get like that, thought John, wondering still that he had never noticed it before. It was certainly lived in, too. He could hear lots of people laughing and dancing to the bagpipe music. Their silhouettes spun backwards and forwards in the windows.

John wondered if he knew any of them; he knew most of the people who lived in the neighbourhood. He wanted very much to go in and join them, but hesitated to knock at the door. He was confident with his friends but shy of strangers. Suppose these people were all strangers. He hovered a few yards away, torn between his shyness and his longing to take part in the music and gaiety.

The door opened.

"Come and join the party, John." The speaker was an old woman. She was a stranger. How did she know his name? She sounded almost as though she was expecting him. John felt anxious. The old woman seemed very friendly; yet there was something about her, the coldness of her eyes perhaps, that made him think it might be better to go back to Black Simon and Patch after all. John took a single step forwards; then he stopped.

The woman beckoned. Then she opened a second door, just inside the house. Beyond that door was the music. It seemed to John that the sound was pounding towards him.

It was taking hold of him and drawing him into the house. He did not want to resist.

Something brushed against his thighs, almost tripping him up. He looked down in alarm. Black Simon was blocking his way. But Black Simon could not thwart him now. He kicked the dog harshly out of his way and entered the house. Simon whimpered, but John did not care. The music was all-powerful.

"I'll take your cap," said the woman. John held it out to her. Her nails were extraordinarily long. Her cold eyes shone, as if she had achieved some triumph.

Black Simon sprang, snapped his huge jaw over the cap, then backed away growling. The spikey fingers grasped thin air. The old woman mumbled something that John did not hear. He knew she was angry, and he was embarrassed by his dog's behaviour.

"I'm very sorry," he said. Her answer reassured him.

"Your cap will be spoiled," she smiled at John. "Come with me. You'll be wanting a drink to warm you." John followed her through the second door.

The room was throbbing with colour and chatter, blending with the fabulous music. But as John entered there was a sudden silence. The people stood still, staring at him. Again he had the feeling he was expected. He glanced shyly about him. He did not know a single face. Moreover, the clothes these strangers wore were unlike anything John had ever seen. They seemed to be made of light rather than cloth, shimmering, flashing light. John found it hard not to blink. It reminded him of coming out of the dark forest into the glare of the midday sun.

Slowly he got used to the dazzling glare. He looked again at the unfamiliar faces. They were beautiful, especially the girls. How he would like to ask one of those girls to dance with him—but he felt so coarse and clumsy in his muddy black oilskins. She would be sure to refuse. She might even laugh at him. If only he could be one of those strange, dazzling men. He wished they would all stop staring at him.

As if in answer to his wish the music started up again. The dancers seemed to forget all about him and turned back to each other. John felt grateful to the musician. He was a great giant of a highland chief, with fiery red hair and black eyes. As John looked across the room at him, he smiled warmly. John smiled back. He felt confident. He was beginning to enjoy himself. The piper went into one of John's favourite tunes. He winked at John. John winked boldly back. The piper nodded to one of the girls. She poured some reddish liquid into a glass and brought it to John.

"Try some of this, John."

She gave him the glass. John sipped cautiously. It tasted a bit like whisky, but more fiery. It excited him. He emptied the glass greedily. "Thank you."

"Would you like another?" the girl smiled. John thought her rather forward; but it was a pleasant change from the village girls, who never opened their mouths unless spoken to.

"Yes, please."

She refilled the glass. He emptied it again, and again, and again. He was feeling gloriously warm and happy now. His exhaustion, hunger and damp all seemed to belong to some other life.

"I like it here," he said. Then he added gallantly, "I like your dress, too."

She looked pleased. He could hardly believe his luck; this beautiful girl actually talking to him, bringing him as many drinks as he wanted, the music, the warmth, the friendly piper. One thing more, and his happiness would be complete: he must dance with this girl to the thrilling music. He only had to ask. Yet something stupid inside him seemed to say, "Don't! You'll regret it!"

"Would . . . would you like to dance?" he stammered.

"I should like that better than anything else in the world." The girl laughed happily. How silly his fears had been. He held out his arms to her.

Something banged hard against his chest, winding him painfully. John found himself clasping Black Simon.

"Get down you brute," he rasped, trying to shake himself free. He staggered beneath the dog's weight and toppled backwards on to the floor.

Everyone was staring again. The room was silent apart from the dog's growls. Only the girl moved. She bent down over John, holding out her hand to help him up. Blearily he looked at her. Lying there, he was mainly aware of her shoes. They reminded him of horses' hooves. He had never seen shoes like that before. Or were they boots? He could not make out where the tops of them were. They seemed to blend with her ankles. Then suddenly John saw they were not boots or shoes. Those hooves were the girl's own feet. The girl was not a human being, nor were any of the people in this house. The piper . . . terrified, John looked across at the piper. He was still smiling, but his smile was no longer friendly. It was horrific, like the grin of a skull. From his silent bagpipes seeped a steady stream of blood. The blood crept across the floor towards John. John scrambled to

JANE EDMONDS

his feet with the desperation of a rabbit caught in a poacher's snare.

"God help me!" he cried.

He was not thinking about God; but in the room his words caused pandemonium. The dancers shrieked and screamed, the air was thick like smoke. There was a terrible stench of sulphur. John thought he would choke. Here and there he glimpsed faces through the fog, but they were not beautiful faces. What he saw were devils.

The air began to clear. Trembling, John looked towards the piper. What he saw made him freeze with terror. The piper was growing and changing before his very eyes. The face was becoming hard and scaly. The eyes, now red, shot sparks of fire. Two great horns were growing out of the forehead. The hands were turning into colossal claws, with nails like cut-throat razors. John knew that this was Satan, chief of all devils. There was no escape: let the Devil take him—only let it be quick!

Then John saw Black Simon hurtling towards the great Devil. John screamed. The Devil raised his claw for the kill. The dog sprang.

"No!" shrieked John. He had to save Black Simon! He wrenched his gun from his shoulder and aimed at the Devil.

The bullet passed straight through his body. There was nothing John could do for Simon now. He turned away. He could not bear to see what was about to happen. He dashed from the room and ran out of the house, tears streaming down his face.

He was safe. But his dog, who had saved his life four times that night, was dead. He had been so stupid and so cruel to Simon. If only he had understood! If only he had had a quarter of the sense of Black Simon! He slowed down to a walk, numb with misery.

Suddenly behind him he heard hooves pounding, a hungry hissing and screeching, coming closer and closer. Satan, followed by a seething mass of devils, was swooping down as if to tear him to pieces. So Simon had not saved him after all, even by dying for him! John broke into a desperate run. He was quite near to the Poacher's Pool. If he could only reach it, he might drown there rather than face the merciless claws of the fiends!

The noise of the hooves was louder. John could hear the devils' hot breath. Flames scorched his back. Another step and he would reach the pool. Again he saw Satan raise his terrible claw.

A cock crew. Night, the time of the Devil's power, was at an end. John fell. The waters of the pool closed over him.

WARM, ROUGH sponges were washing his face. Warily John opened his eyes. Dogs! Big black dogs were licking his face. One had a white patch on its chest, and the other . . . John stared in wonder at the silky throat. Below the throat were four white hairs—to keep the Devil from harming him, the village people would say. So Black Simon was alive. The village people were right! John felt a great wave of relief and happiness. Simon's white hairs had saved him! John raised his head slightly. He gave a little gasp of pain. His neck and shoulders felt raw. He looked down at his oilskin coat. It was singed and tattered. His arms, poking through remains of sleeves, were purple and red. When he moved them he felt a burning pain. The rest of his body was ice-cold and wet. Dimly John remembered running towards the Poacher's Pool, the feel of cold water engulfing him. He turned his sore neck to one side. He was lying right next to the pool.

Why was he not lying down there, in the water, drowned among the reeds like the poacher who had given the pool its name? What miracle had saved him?

Black Simon shook himself, spraying water drops in all directions. John's question was answered.

2

The Rings That Burned

HIS CORN-COLOURED hair streamed in the wind as he ran down the slope towards the village, clutching his lute. To the girls he looked like a god. They came running from all directions: big girls, little girls, thin girls, fat girls, ugly girls, pretty girls, clever girls, stupid girls. They were not supposed to go near him; but they all did. Their parents said he was a lazy good-for-nothing. But the girls knew better. For Paul sang to them. Paul smiled so beautifully at them that they felt their hearts would burst.

Yvonne joined the other girls. She did not run or shout, but walked primly, tossing her head from time to time to show off her shimmering fair hair. She did not like to be one of the crowd. She was offended that Paul did not single her out, when secretly she idolized him like the rest of the girls. In her eyes his only fault was that he did not notice her. Everybody else did. Everybody else said she was the most beautiful girl in the village.

Yvonne's mother, the widow Margot, never allowed her

to forget her beauty. She felt it was important that a girl should know her own value.

"You can have the best husband in Brittany," she said over and over again. Yvonne believed her.

In truth, neither of them knew much about the Brittany beyond their village. But they had both chosen the man who they thought would be "the best husband in Brittany". For Yvonne he was the handsomest man in the neighbourhood, the husband who would turn all the other girls green with envy: Paul. For Madame Margot he was simply the richest man in the neighbourhood, the husband who would turn all the other mothers green with envy: Monsieur Charlot.

Monsieur Charlot was a farmer. He was forty-two years old with a swollen nose and a stomach that wobbled like a jelly. He smelled slightly of manure on Sunday, after his weekly wash, and strongly of manure all the rest of the week. It was understood by the widow Margot and Monsieur Charlot that he was to marry Yvonne on her sixteenth birthday. They hadn't mentioned their plans to Yvonne herself.

Yvonne was to be sixteen in a month. Standing there in the street, listening to the haunting twang of Paul's lute, she began to make plans of her own.

The first thing was to find Paul alone and speak to him away from the crowd of stupid girls that always surrounded him in the village; she had to force him to notice her. So the next day, very early in the morning, Yvonne slipped out of her house and ran across the fields towards the sea shore.

The beach was deserted, except for an old fisherman who sat huddled over a net he was mending. His ragged coat flapped in the wind. He was so gnarled and weatherbeaten that he seemed to belong more to the craggy rocks than to the human race. He leered at Yvonne. His gums were toothless, decaying. She turned away with a shudder. She hated poor, ugly things. The old man broke into a hideous, mocking cackle. Then abruptly he stopped laughing and spoke.

"You think you are beautiful, but when you are vain and selfish your soul is ugly—as ugly as I am!"

Yvonne stared at him, horrified. How could he say such a terrible thing? Was he mad? The old man grinned maliciously.

"My master likes your kind. If you are not careful he will come for you." The old man's body began to shake wildly, and once again he began to cackle with laughter. His words made no sense to Yvonne. The ghastly old man must be a lunatic. Frightened, she turned and hurried away along the beach.

To her relief she saw Paul walking straight towards her.

"Listen!" He held out a large shell that curled inwards like a fist. "Put it to your ear. It makes music."

Yvonne was not one to miss a good opportunity.

"You hold it for me. I might not do it properly." She looked into Paul's eyes as he held the shell close to her ear. The crazy old fisherman was forgotten. Now he can see that I am beautiful, she thought. The shell made a buzzing, watery sound.

"Can you hear the music?" Paul asked eagerly.

"Yes. It's lovely," Yvonne answered to please him. She smiled her most dazzling smile. She felt sure that Paul would single her out from now on.

It was late afternoon when Yvonne crept back into the house, fearful lest her mother should see the glow on her cheeks. Her expedition had been a triumph. Paul had kissed her. He had told her that she was beautiful. They had arranged to meet again on the following day. A little shiver of excitement ran down her spine at the thought of how jealous the other girls would be if they knew.

"Yvonne! Come in here. We have a visitor." Her mother's voice from the best room punctured her happy dream. She must have been listening for her. Yvonne smoothed down her wind-blown hair and went into the room. There was a smell of manure.

Monsieur Charlot heaved himself out of the best chair. He gave Yvonne a slobbery kiss.

"My bride," he said. Yvonne burst into tears and rushed out of the room.

"It is too much emotion," the widow Margot explained to Monsieur Charlot. "She is overwhelmed by the great honour that you do her."

So the wedding was settled. Monsieur Charlot went away satisfied, if a little puzzled by his fiancée's extraordinary behaviour at the news of her engagement.

AT FIRST Yvonne tried to change her mother's mind. She told her that she found Monsieur Charlot revolting, that she would rather die than marry him. Madame Margot told her daughter that Monsieur Charlot was the best husband in Brittany; there was no question of her changing her mind. So Yvonne went to bed and refused to eat. Her mother tried to tempt her with her favourite food—wild strawberries and cream; Yvonne just threw the plate at her. On the third day the widow was beginning to be worried that Yvonne might make herself seriously ill, but she still refused to give in. Monsieur Charlot was the best husband in Brittany. Yvonne *must* marry him.

However, her worry turned out to be unnecessary. On the fourth day Yvonne appeared to see reason. She sat up in bed, said she would be quite happy to get married, ate her strawberries and cream greedily, and then told her mother that she was going for a walk.

When Yvonne returned from her walk she was smiling happily. Her cheeks glowed brightly. When Monsieur Charlot arrived with a present of a large goat's cheese she thanked him politely. She began to take an interest in the satin wedding dress that her mother and the two maids were making for her at Monsieur Charlot's expense. She did not want to go and play with her village friends any more. Her mother assumed that Yvonne felt above such childish occupations, now that she was shortly to be married. She preferred to go for walks, from which she always returned glowing and smiling.

The eve of the wedding arrived. Madame Margot noticed with delight that Yvonne was happier and more beautiful than ever before. She had been right to insist on this marriage. Monsieur Charlot was the best husband in Brittany.

As soon as it was dusk, Yvonne said, "I think I'll go to bed now. I want to look my best tomorrow." She kissed her mother more affectionately than usual. She is sad to be leaving me, thought Madame Margot.

Madame Margot was right; Yvonne was sad, for she thought she would not see her mother again. She went upstairs, and very quietly slipped into her wedding dress. She gazed at herself admiringly in the glass. She listened to her mother moving around the house for a while, giving final instructions to the maids about the wedding feast. Then the house fell silent. A soft, haunting twang broke the silence. Her husband was outside, waiting for her.

AT A QUARTER to eleven the following morning the bells were ringing gaily. The villagers hurried towards the church. The bridegroom, his stomach squeezed into a new velvet jerkin, was standing in the front pew, clutching the wedding ring in his sweating hand and looking nervously at the priest. Soon the church was full.

The old fisherman could find nowhere to sit, so he huddled in a corner, unnoticed.

The bells went on ringing, on and on. People were beginning to look round expectantly for the bride.

"The widow Margot is here." "Yvonne must be coming now." "Madame Margot looks agitated." "She is crying!" "What can be the matter?"

The widow hurried down the aisle towards Monsieur Charlot and clutched him feverishly by the hand.

"Yvonne is gone! And she has taken her wedding dress!" Monsieur Charlot stared at her in disbelief; but her face told him that she was not lying. His look changed to one of fury and misery. He flung the wedding ring down on the floor and marched out of the church. The villagers bustled out of the church in a flurry of excitement and scandal. Monsieur Charlot was never seen again.

As soon as he was alone, the old fisherman crept out of his corner and picked up the ring. Leering triumphantly, he slipped it on to his horny, stick-like finger. His master would be pleased. A hideous mirthless cackle filled the church.

YVONNE AND PAUL had planned to get married immediately after Yvonne's escape. They set out, full of excitement and hope, in search of a priest who would marry them for a few sous. But there was no such priest to be found. Yvonne tore her beautiful wedding dress on a thorn. It started to rain. Mud splashed on to the white dress. They were both soaked to the skin. Yvonne was glad that her friends could not see her now. Paul, who had seemed such a romantic figure, now appeared bedraggled and feeble. She was angry that he managed things so badly.

After a day's trudging they managed to find shelter in a convent. It was hardly the answer to their dreams, but it was better than shivering in the rain. The nuns were kind; they took Yvonne in and let Paul spend the night in the cowshed. The next day Paul left to seek his fortune. He promised faithfully to return as soon as he had earned enough money to make Yvonne happy. Yvonne promised faithfully to wait for him. There was nothing else she could do.

Three months passed. The convent was very dreary. Nobody ever laughed or sang or even spoke above a whisper, except in the chapel. The food was dull; she had to go to mass three times a day; and she had to work for her keep, spoiling the soft hands her mother had treasured so carefully, sewing rough cloth and picking fruit that blackened her nails. Yvonne was very unhappy.

Then one day a young gentleman called Bertrand came to the convent to discuss the sale of some land. The first thing he saw on entering the gardens was Yvonne, gazing mournfully at the fruit trees. She was wearing a sack-cloth dress the nuns had given her. Her long fair hair shone in the sunlight. Her face was pale as ivory. Her eyes, glistening with tears, were a deep blue, like the sea. He thought that he had never seen a girl look so sad and so beautiful.

"Mademoiselle." Yvonne looked up. There was the finest man she had ever seen. Not only was he young and good looking, but he was wearing a rich suit of dark red velvet and a cloak embroidered with gold. He was bowing to her.

Hurriedly she tried to hide her blackened hands behind her back, but the man was too quick for her. He caught them in his own white hands and gazed down at them.

"It is sad to spoil your lovely hands." Yvonne smiled wistfully. Paul would never have said such a thing.

"Tell me why you do this work," said Bertrand gently. So Yvonne told him her story—how her mother had tried to force her to marry a loathsome farmer, how she had run away with Paul, and how Paul had cruelly abandoned her in this convent. Bertrand was deeply moved by her tale of woe. He decided then and there to marry her and make her happy.

Bertrand drove Yvonne away from the convent in a carriage. She was wearing a blue satin dress sewn with pearls which he had given her. It was far more splendid than her wedding dress. Yvonne compared this triumphant departure with her sad arrival. She was pleased with herself. Bertrand was taking her back to her mother. She was confident that her mother would also be pleased with her.

The widow Margot could hardly believe her eyes when she saw her daughter step down from a carriage at the front gate. She forgave Yvonne everything and gave the happy couple her blessing. Bertrand was surely the best husband in Brittany.

Two days later Paul arrived at the convent door. He had earned a little money by his singing and had brought back a finely-made harp which would help him to earn more, and a gold wedding ring. He was longing for the moment when he could place the ring on Yvonne's finger. That moment had almost arrived, he thought. But the Mother Superior told him that Yvonne had returned home and was to be married to Bertrand. Paul left her without saying a word.

He walked without stopping until he reached Yvonne's house. Watched only by an old fisherman, he put his new harp on the ground outside her door; he trod on it; then jumped on it, again and again until it was smashed into a hundred pieces. Beside the fragments he carefully placed the golden wedding ring. Then he walked away, his corn-coloured hair fluttering limply in the breeze, down towards the sea shore.

As soon as he was out of sight, the old fisherman sidled slowly up to the house and picked up the ring. Chuckling malevolently, he slid it on to his finger where it chinked gently against Yvonne's other unused wedding ring.

"Only one more," he muttered, grinning to himself, "then she will belong to my master."

Paul was never seen again.

THE VILLAGE people were looking forward to Yvonne's wedding with mixed feelings. It was to be a splendid party for them all, with feasting and dancing for five days. However, the men were sorry to see a beautiful girl going to someone else; the mothers were annoyed that Yvonne, who had behaved so wickedly, had made such a catch; and the daughters could only think of Paul, and blame Yvonne bitterly for his disappearance.

Even the widow Margot's happiness was marred by a disturbing event. She was walking home glorying in the thought that her daughter had now really found the best husband in Brittany, when an ugly old fisherman with no teeth suddenly blocked her path and thrust something into her hand.

"Pity to go to the expense of a wedding ring when she's got two already," he mocked. The widow screamed. Her hand was burning. She opened it and two gold rings fell to the ground. The fisherman picked up the rings.

"That's how Hell burns. You tell your daughter," he cackled as he limped away. In spite of her delight over the wedding, Madame Margot could not forget this incident. She said nothing to Yvonne, but decided to keep a close watch on her, even sharing her bedroom, until the wedding had actually started.

THE GREAT day arrived. Yvonne looked radiant in her dress of white velvet embroidered with silver, over which she wore a golden cloak. Ten bridesmaids in pale pink velvet were to follow her to the church. The widow breathed a sigh of relief as she watched the procession wind gracefully down the lane. She arranged her own black satin dress, put on her veil, and admired herself for a moment before she set out to catch them up. Her own and her daughter's happiness were now certain.

It was a silent procession. The bridesmaids had once been Yvonne's friends; but she had taken away Paul, then cast him off like an old boot. They could find nothing to say to her now. She felt their dislike and knew the reason, but her heart was full of her husband-to-be and her new life as a grand lady. Soon it would not matter. Every step was taking her nearer to Bertrand.

Suddenly Yvonne stopped. The other girls drew back, afraid. The way was blocked by a knight on a black horse. He dismounted and stepped towards Yvonne. Beams of sunlight glanced off his steel breast-plate, his golden helmet glittered. Yvonne stared at him in wonder. He took off his helmet. His eyes met hers. The power of his eyes was almost unbearable. Yvonne felt them pulling her towards him. She knew she must resist them. Bertrand would be waiting at the church. She turned away from those eyes, towards her bridesmaids.

"Help me!" she gasped.

The girls stood motionless, half-mocking, half-afraid. The knight spoke almost in a whisper.

"I am a king. I will take you to my kingdom if you consent to be mine."

Bertrand, a minute ago so clear and important in her mind, faded to a shadow. Yvonne stepped forward into the arms of the wonderful knight. He lifted her on to his horse and leapt up behind her. In a moment they were gone.

BERTRAND STOOD at the front of the church, the wedding ring in his hand. The priest paced backwards and forwards nervously. The bride was late. He was reminded uncomfortably of the last time he was supposed to marry her. He heard whispers among the congregation. Now Bertrand was turning round wondering what they were saying. The bells rang and rang. Someone in the church chuckled. Someone else bet a dozen eggs that Yvonne would not turn up. The old fisherman, huddled unnoticed in the corner, watched knowingly.

Voices became clearer. "Didn't I say so?" "She's a wicked girl." "You owe me a dozen eggs."

Then, one by one, the people began to leave the church, till only Bertrand, the priest and the old fisherman remained.

"You'd better go home, my son," the priest told Bertrand gently. "I do not understand your fiancée; I think she may be in the Devil's clutches."

A cackling laugh echoed through the church. Bertrand turned round and saw the old fisherman shaking with crazy laughter. Wild with humiliation and misery he rushed at the old man and gave him a violent blow on the head with his clenched fist. The fisherman fell in a heap of rags upon the floor. The ring that Bertrand had been holding clattered to the floor beside him. Bertrand ran out of the church past the groups of gossiping villagers, past the frightened bridesmaids who had arrived to tell their story, past the weeping form of Madame Margot. The villagers stared at him with pity. They knew that they would never see him again.

THE BLACK HORSE galloped across the sea shore. The warrior king held tightly to Yvonne. The sun lit up his armour and her wedding gown. Yvonne's heart pounded with excitement. She knew there had never been such a splendid couple. Her mother had said that she could have the best husband in Brittany, but she could never have dreamed that Yvonne would marry a king.

A long, narrow boat with a black sail was waiting a little way out to sea. The horse stepped through the waves towards it. Curiously, the water never seemed to come higher than its ankles. It was as if they were riding over the surface of the water.

The horse stepped so lightly into the boat that it did not even rock. The knight dismounted and lifted Yvonne down on to some black silken cushions. An old servant took the horse's bridle. Yvonne was surprised at his appearance. He looked so ragged and hunched; he had no teeth. He was not at all her idea of a king's servant. Also there was something familiar about him, as if she had seen him before somewhere —but she could not remember. His master spoke to him.

"Have you got all three?" The old man handed him something. Yvonne thought she heard the chink of metal.

The boat slid slowly out of the bay. It seemed that night

JANE EDMONDS

was falling already. The sea was black and strangely still. The air suddenly felt cold. Yvonne began to shiver. She did not like this part of the journey at all.

"It is very far to your kingdom?" she asked the warrior anxiously.

"Not for you." It was an odd reply but Yvonne was happy that the journey would soon be over. She was freezing now. Her teeth began to chatter. The night had become completely dark. Yvonne felt better if she kept talking.

"I've never been to sea at night before."

"This is not the sea. This is not the night."

Yvonne felt a sudden surge of fear. How could this not be the sea or the night? Her mouth felt dry. She had difficulty in speaking.

"Where . . .?" The knight cut her short.

"It is the Lake of Anguish. It leads to my kingdom." He smiled greedily. "Now is the moment for you to become my bride." His eyes shone like coals in the darkness. They were more powerful than ever. Yvonne knew that she had to obey those eyes, even though now they filled her heart not with excitement but with terror.

"Give me your hand, so that I may put your wedding ring on your finger." Yvonne held out her hand towards the knight. He took it. She felt a searing agony in her fourth finger. She jerked her hand away. But the pain only grew fiercer. She looked down: on her finger were three gold rings, burning deep into her flesh.

"They are all meant for you," mocked the knight, "one from each forsaken husband." He began to laugh. "But there's no chance that you'll forsake your fourth husband. My brides never forsake *me*."

Desperately Yvonne clutched at her burning finger, trying

to wrench off the torturing rings. It was no use. The knight laughed louder. Yvonne fell back on the cushions defeated.

Immediately horny hands seized her by the head and jerked her forward. She found herself staring into the hideous face of the old servant. He was leering at her, displaying toothless, decaying gums. She felt sick. She knew now where she had seen him before—a crazy old fisherman huddled on the sea shore. What he had said then, forgotten so lightly, was ringing in her head now over and over again: *"Your soul is ugly—as ugly as I am . . . my master likes your kind . . . he will come for you . . ."* the jangle of words tortured her brain like a fever.

The old man pulled her head closer to his own and gazed into her eyes.

"My master is the Devil," he said.

Yvonne felt her head thud back on to the cushions. The old man vanished. Above her now loomed only the sinister black silhouette of his master.

Beyond him something was gleaming, white. Faces? As the boat drew nearer Yvonne saw that they were not faces but skulls, grimacing, tormented: millions of them stretching endlessly into the darkness.

"This is where my kingdom begins," said the Devil. Yvonne buried her face in the cushions. She did not want to see any more. The boat entered the mouth of Hell. An appalling wail filled the air, and Yvonne's fingers, her hands, her whole body, burned.

3

The Devil's Cats

ALEXANDER FRAZER drank his whisky very, very slowly. He was reluctant to leave the friendly inn and continue his round of this mean little grey village. He came into Scrabster every week to collect the rents from his tenants; it was never a very pleasant task, but this week it was likely to be especially unpleasant. He was going to tell Madge Olson that she must leave her cottage.

Madge Olson was a sallow, scraggy woman with narrow green eyes and tight lips. She looked, and was, poor and mean. Frazer found her repulsive. But this was not his reason for getting rid of her.

Madge had paid no rent for six months now, and, worse still, she kept removing bits of the cottage and selling them; only last week Frazer had noticed that all the brass door-knobs had disappeared; the previous week it had been the fireplace. He had found a new tenant for the cottage, a stonemason called William Montgomery who badly needed somewhere to live, as he had a wife and three children. Frazer felt he was right to evict Madge Olson, but she had a violent temper which would have no time for rights or wrongs. He wished fervently that this evening were over.

As it wasn't, he decided to put off the awful moment a little longer and have another whisky. The landlord was almost reluctant to serve him; he was absorbed in a discussion with some local fishermen, which they carried on in hushed, secretive tones. Frazer could not resist eavesdropping.

"He was outside Margaret Nin-Gilbert's house. I saw him with my own eyes—a huge black horse, ten feet tall!" A tall story, joked Frazer to himself. The fishermen were discussing one of their favourite topics—the Devil. Frazer didn't believe a word of it.

"He comes to see Margaret Nin-Gilbert," whispered a fisherman. Frazer almost laughed out loud. Margaret was one of his best tenants, kind and motherly, with plump arms and rosy cheeks, and wispy grey hair escaping from a floppy bun.

"You'll be saying she's a witch next!" he mocked. The fishermen's response astounded him. They seemed quite to forget his rank, and turned on him with passionate earnestness.

"How else does she know how to cure people? How did she become a midwife?" they demanded.

"She knows something about herbs and medicine, that's all," replied Frazer reasonably.

"And what about her charms? She once killed a baby by putting a spell on its mother."

"New-born babies do sometimes die. You cannot blame her. She is a good midwife." Frazer was beginning to get angry. Really, the stupidity of these fishermen!

"She has red spots on her arms," they argued.

"Birthmarks!" retorted Frazer.

"Witch's marks, made by the Devil!"

"If you go on with this sort of talk, Scrabster will lose a good midwife," said Frazer. Did these silly men not realize that if the sheriff of Caithness or someone in authority were to hear about this, poor Margaret could be arrested and burned to death?

"She can turn herself into a cat!" cried one of the men. This was the final straw. It was hopeless arguing with such simpletons. Frazer gulped down his whisky and left the inn.

As it happened, his first call was to Margaret Nin-Gilbert. He rapped on the door. She seemed to be out—again. This was the third week. Could she not pay her rent? It was unlikely. Frazer knew that she was rarely short of money. She did well out of her midwifery and her herbal cures. He decided to wait a few minutes to see if she would come back. He was happy to put off the visit to Madge Olson as long as possible. He leaned comfortably against the porch and admired the night. There was a full moon, which lit up the bare, wintry trees. Everything was silent apart from the faint murmur of the sea in the distance.

He was startled by a rustling of dry leaves. He stood quite still, his heart pounding.

When he saw what had frightened him, he wanted to burst out laughing. It was only a large black cat. The cat ran across to Margaret's cottage, leapt on to the sill of a slightly open window, and disappeared from view. Frazer, feeling rather foolish, set off towards the next house. As he turned into the lane, he happened to glance back over his shoulder. There was a candle burning in one of Margaret's windows.

Frazer felt angry. She must have been hiding inside all the time, pretending to be out in order to avoid paying the rent. Well, he'd soon see about that! He marched back to the house and knocked very loudly. If she didn't answer . . .

But Margaret came to the door immediately. She curtsied politely.

"Oh Mr Frazer, you'll be wanting your rent." She fetched a jar from the mantelpiece and counted out the three weeks' money she owed him. Frazer noticed there was plenty left in the jar. There was obviously no problem about paying the rent. Nor did she seem in the least unwilling to do so. Yet she must have been in there hiding from him for some reason. He had been standing right by the porch and would have seen her if she had come in.

"I'm sorry there's two weeks overdue. I've been out rather often just lately."

"You were out when I called a few minutes ago," said Frazer, wondering what she would say to that.

"That's right." A plain blatant lie. Why was she lying to him?

Frazer soon forgot about the mystery of Margaret Nin-Gilbert in his concern over his next call—Madge Olson's cottage. All his fears were justified. It was a very unpleasant experience. Madge screamed and stamped and cursed him. She threw onions at him and some roof-tiles—probably intended for sale this week, he thought. However he stood firm. She must be out in a week's time or he would have her arrested.

As soon as Mr Frazer was out of sight, Madge Olson slipped out of her cottage and went to see her neighbour, Margaret Nin-Gilbert. Margaret listened awkwardly to her tale of woe. She suspected Madge had some favour to ask, and that it would be a favour she had no wish to grant.

"Just because he is wealthy and I'm a poor woman he thinks he can do just as he likes," whined Madge, "and the trouble is, he's right, unless somebody can help me." She paused and looked meaningfully at Margaret.

"I don't see what I can do," replied Margaret.

"But you're the only person who can do something," wheedled Madge. "You can put a spell on Mr Frazer, so that he won't be able to turn me out." Her green eyes glinted maliciously.

So that was it. Why should she put a spell on Mr Frazer? She liked him. She had always found him a good and fair landlord. He was probably quite right to evict Madge. She shook her head.

Madge stood up, furious. She was about to storm out when she noticed Margaret staring straight past her, out of the window. Her rosy cheeks were drained of all their colour. Her hands were shaking. What was she looking at that so terrified her? Madge's eyes followed hers.

There outside, like a vast grim shadow, stood a black horse. Madge shivered with wonder and terror, her anger forgotten. The horse was at least ten feet tall. In the dusk its whole body gleamed as if it were standing in a bright light. It turned its head to gaze at her. Its eyes were like great black pools that suck people down into their depths. Madge wanted to drown in those eyes. She took a step towards the window.

Margaret spoke, her voice trembling.

"I'll do what I can." The black horse faded into the night. Madge turned back to Margaret.

"Was that him?" she whispered, hissing with excitement. Margaret nodded.

Madge's eyes gleamed triumphantly. "He made you change your mind about Mr Frazer?"

"Yes!" snapped Margaret.

"So he's on my side!"

Margaret stared searchingly at Madge's mean, sharp little face. "I think he wants you," she said.

A WEEK later Alexander Frazer was riding towards Scrabster to see if Madge Olson had obeyed his orders to leave the cottage. As he was coming up to the bridge that led into the village, his horse stumbled. Frazer managed to save it from falling, but the horse was frightened. It stood stock still, shaking violently. Frazer tried to urge it on, but it refused to move. Then Frazer tried giving it a gentle tap with his whip. The horse broke into a frenzy, rearing and frothing at the mouth. Frazer clung on for all he was worth; the animal must tire soon. But the horse did not tire. The battle raged on, man and beast becoming more and more desperate. Frazer's arms and legs ached. He knew he would soon have to let go. He felt himself go limp. He fell. The horse reared up again, and again. It was only a matter of seconds till his hooves would come down on Frazer if he did not manage to crawl out of the way. He tried to raise himself, but was too exhausted to move. He could only wait to be trampled to death.

"God have mercy on my soul," he whispered, then closed his eyes and waited for the crushing blow of the horse's hooves.

It did not come. Slowly he opened his eyes. There was his horse standing beside him, quite placid. He could not believe it; relief and joy flowed back into his whole being. He felt his strength return.

Very gingerly Frazer got up. His body felt strained and bruised, but he was not seriously hurt. He took his horse's bridle, mounted and rode across the bridge.

He stopped at the inn before going to Madge's cottage. His narrow escape had left him feeling shaky. He needed to talk about it to someone, even if it was only the fishermen. They listened to his story in awed silence. When he had finished, one of them spoke.

"Mark my words, sir, that was witchcraft."

"You and your witches!" laughed Frazer. "I don't believe a word of it." But he felt even more shaky than before.

Madge, confident that Margaret Nin-Gilbert's spell would succeed, had not moved out of the cottage. Frazer was surprised that she dared defy him. She seemed taken aback and angry to see him. Looking at her pointed snarling face and her hard green eyes glittering with hatred, he thought that she would make a much better witch than the fishermen's famous Nin-Gilbert. He gave Madge one more day to get out. Tomorrow morning he would return with the constable.

Secretly, Margaret Nin-Gilbert was glad when Madge Olson came storming round to tell her that her spell had been useless. She had done all she could. Her master the Devil could not blame her if Mr Frazer had found some way of protecting himself, and he would not expect her to attack such a difficult target again.

"You'd better just do as you're told, and move out," she told Madge, hoping her voice did not sound too triumphant. Madge obviously thought it did.

"You're not fit to serve the Devil!" she shrieked, dancing

with rage. "Let him come to me! I'll show him! I'll show you! I'll show Mr Frazer! You'll all be sorry!"

That night Madge Olson met the black horse.

WILLIAM MONTGOMERY and his family were delighted with their new home. It had a huge room downstairs and two upstairs, one for William and his wife Jane, the other for the three children, Andrew, Johnnie, and the baby Helen. They replaced the doorknobs and the fireplace and William put new tiles on the roof. It seemed to them a palace. The only sad thing was that William had to go away down to Perth, as there was no work for him nearer.

He left one Sunday evening, to be at work first thing on Monday morning. Jane stood in the porch waving goodbye; Andrew aged eight and little Johnnie aged five, stood on either side of her. William looked back at them anxiously. He didn't like leaving them.

"Take care of your mother for me, Andrew!" he shouted.

"I will," Andrew yelled back proudly. William's horse rounded the corner and mother and children went inside.

If William had known what was going to happen that night, he would have liked leaving even less.

THE CHILDREN were in bed. Jane was downstairs by the fire, sewing a nightdress for Helen. Suddenly a small figure appeared at the top of the stairs.

"Mother, there's a cat under my bed." It was Johnnie. He spoke in a tiny frightened whisper.

"Don't be silly Johnnie, you know there are no cats in the house." Jane was kind but firm.

"Mother, there is!" Johnnie was beginning to cry. He looked white as a ghost. Jane got up and went upstairs. He must have had a bad dream, poor little boy. She picked him up and carried him into his room. She tucked him back into bed beside Andrew, who was sleeping soundly, and sang to him. In a few minutes he was asleep. She crept out of the room and went back to her sewing.

The next night the same thing happened, only this time Johnnie was too frightened to go back to sleep. He just lay quietly and stiffly in the bed. Jane sat with him till she was fit to drop, then crept away to her own bed. Johnnie did not try to stop her; he just lay there, frozen with fear.

Johnnie saw the cat every night for a week. He could not sleep. He could not eat. He scarcely even spoke. His eyes had great black circles around them. His ribs and joints stuck out so that he began to look more like a skeleton than a boy of five. Jane was desperately worried. She decided to ask her neighbour, Margaret Nin-Gilbert, if she knew of any medicine to cure bad dreams.

Margaret was strangely curious about Johnnie's dream. What colour was the cat? Was Jane quite certain that there wasn't a cat in the house? Nevertheless she said she would have some medicine ready for the next day—on one condition; tonight Jane must make sure that the cat was not real, by looking under the bed herself.

That night, Jane tucked Johnnie back into bed as usual. He felt pathetically light in her arms. She sang to him as usual, and he lay stiff and silent as usual. Jane kissed him sadly.

"If I look under the bed and I don't find anything, will you believe then that there is no cat?" she said. Johnnie did not reply. He just watched her. He knew.

Jane lifted the side of the bedcover and peered underneath. Two hard green eyes glittered at her out of the shadow. The room went black. Jane fell to the floor in a dead faint.

THAT WAS how Alexander Frazer found her when he came to collect the rent the next day. Johnnie was sitting beside her, staring into space as if petrified with horror. Andrew had a cloth and was sponging his mother's forehead. Frazer took Jane's wrist. Thank goodness! He could still feel her pulse beating gently.

Leaving the stricken cottage, he hurried round to see Margaret Nin-Gilbert. She would know what to do.

Margaret did not seem surprised by his visit. She picked up a large bottle of red-brown cordial almost as if she had been waiting, and followed Frazer back to the Montgomery cottage. When she saw Jane lying on the floor she turned very pale. She knelt down beside her without saying a word, and began first to pour the cordial very slowly into her mouth, then to massage her cold body.

"What about the boy?" Frazer looked at Johnnie, who still had not moved from his horror-struck, staring position.

"Put him back to bed! Then give him some of my medicine!" Margaret seemed to know what she was doing, and Frazer was grateful to her. He took Johnnie in his arms. As he did so the little body relaxed and the head lolled back sharply on to Frazer's arm. Was he dead?

"Cat!" The child shrieked suddenly. Frazer breathed a sigh of relief. "Cat! Cat! Cat! Cat! . . ." the wild scream continued. Margaret Nin-Gilbert leapt across to the bed and held the bottle of cordial to Johnnie's distorted mouth. He was silent. A moment later he fell into a deep, heavy sleep.

Jane sat up and spoke.

"There was a cat," she said, "a big grey cat. It had green eyes".

THAT EVENING Margaret Nin-Gilbert visited Madge Olson. Madge now lived in an old ruined cottage a little way out of the village. When she saw Margaret her green eyes sparkled.

"You never told me it was such fun," she said. "You should have seen her."

"So it was you?" Margaret had really known ever since Jane had first told her about Johnnie's dream.

"Yes!" hissed Madge. "They think they can take my house!" She began to laugh horribly.

"But you can't blame that poor woman and her children; blame Mr Frazer . . ."

"I shall get them all," interrupted Madge. "You're not the only witch in Scrabster now."

"I can fight you," retorted Margaret.

"And what about our master?" Madge pointed through the broken doorway, smiling confidently. Margaret turned—and saw the black horse, looming in the darkness before her like a gigantic inescapable threat.

ALEXANDER FRAZER went as usual to the inn after he had finished his rent collecting. He ordered a whisky and sat down by himself in a corner. He wanted to decide what he should do about the Montgomery family. He had no idea what was going on, but he had a sickening fear for them. He felt some terror hovering in the background. And yet it was all so absurd. A big grey cat! What was so special about a big grey cat? He knew what the fishermen on the other side of the room would say. Witchcraft! He didn't want to hear it. He decided to keep his story to himself. Nevertheless he thought it might be useful to go and have a chat with Margaret Nin-Gilbert.

He met her in the lane outside her house. She looked distressed and frightened.

"I was just on my way to thank you for your help this morning," he told her. Margaret looked up at him sadly.

"You can't depend on me any more," she said.

"Surely there's no need." Frazer examined her face suspiciously. "Mrs Montgomery is quite well again now." Margaret took no notice of what he said.

"You must send for her husband," she whispered urgently.

"Why should I do that?" Frazer thought that he might be on the point of discovering something. But Margaret did not answer. "Why?" repeated Frazer sharply. "I want to know the reason." Margaret still made no reply. It was as if she did not hear or see him. She was gazing into the darkness beyond. Frazer turned to see what had so caught her attention.

What he saw made his blood turn cold—a huge black horse about ten feet tall; the horse the fisherman had described!

Then he heard the door shutting. Margaret had gone into her house. He went after her and knocked, but there was no reply. Half an hour later Frazer was riding towards Perth, to fetch William Montgomery.

On his way he tried to piece things together. It was becoming difficult to dismiss the fishermen's talk about witchcraft. There was no doubt that Margaret Nin-Gilbert knew more than she was telling. He himself had seen a black cat enter her house only two weeks ago. A cat was haunting the Montgomery's cottage. Now tonight he had seen the horse, with his own eyes, ten feet tall, just as the fisherman had described.

Yet something did not quite fit. If Margaret were a witch, serving the Devil and persecuting the Montgomery family, why was she so concerned about them?

PERHAPS IT had just been a terrible nightmare, thought Jane. She felt quite calm now in the cool darkness. The children were sleeping heavily and she too felt drowsy. Margaret Nin-Gilbert had told her to give them each a spoonful of cordial before putting them to bed, and to take some herself at the same time. Jane decided not to sew that night. She would just go and sit in the children's room for a few minutes before going to bed. She sat down on the end of John and Andrew's bed, content to see them so safely asleep. Her eyelids felt heavy; she just could not be bothered to move. She let her head sink down. After a good sleep she would be quite all right again.

Then something sprang on to the bed. Something furry brushed past her face. She heard Andrew scream. She sat up. She saw the grey cat sitting on Andrew's chest, its green eyes glinting. Andrew was struggling uselessly beneath its weight. Jane felt giddy, but she must not faint. She must save Andrew. She grabbed the cat by its ears and flung it across the room. The cat gave a howl of pain, a howl that sounded almost human. Suddenly Andrew leapt out of bed. He was screaming again. Jane saw a second grey cat spring across the pillow towards Johnnie. She was too far away to stop it. She covered her eyes with her hands. Then she heard a second weird human howl of pain. Andrew had caught the cat by the tail and was pulling it away from his small

ANE EDMONDS.

brother. Jane lunged forward and gave the cat a vicious swipe across the neck.

Almost immediately she heard a cackle of laughter behind her. A third cat was perched on the edge of the baby's cradle. It was about to spring down on to little Helen's face. It would kill her. But Jane knew she could fight now. She picked up the jug from the washstand and brought it down on the cat's head. The cat fell to the floor. The other two disappeared. The battle was over. For the second time Jane lost consciousness.

Her husband and Frazer arrived at dawn. This time Frazer did not fetch Margaret Nin-Gilbert. He no longer trusted her.

William Montgomery stayed at home for nearly a fortnight. At first his wife was too ill to look after the children, even though all three of them were unusually quiet and subdued. They did not even want to eat. The boys did not get their clothes dirty like they normally did, for they seemed to have no energy to go tree-climbing or play outlaws in the mud and bushes. William felt very worried about them.

But there was no sign of the grey cats, and, little by little, Jane and the children began to look better and recover their spirits. William began to be more worried about losing his job in Perth than the cats. At last Jane persuaded him that he should go back to work. It seemed that she and the children had only been having nightmares. They were probably nervous because he was away. If the cats had been real they would not have stopped coming just because he was at home.

Out in her ruined cottage, Madge Olson was nursing some very bad bruises and a pair of twisted ears. In Scrabster itself a woman died of a head wound, in which were found some splinters of china. A third woman had been unable to sit down for a week. Madge had even more reason to get her revenge now. When she saw the black horse, she told him that she needed more help.

Jane was not going to have any more nightmares. She was determined not to. The night William went away, she went about the house cheerfully, singing to herself for company. Occasionally she popped into the children's room just to make sure that they weren't lying awake scared.

She stood there listening contentedly to their regular breathing. How stupid she had been, she thought.

A sudden pain stabbed into her shin. She looked down and saw a grey claw ripping through her flesh. She jerked her leg away, crying out in agony. Then the cat flung itself at her shoulder and bit savagely into her neck. The room blurred. Jane could hear human voices and laughter. Was the pain driving her crazy? There were no people there; only grey cat-like creatures that danced before her tear-filled eyes.

Suddenly she heard the children crying out in terror. Cats were swarming across the bed and the cradle. Forgetting the animal still fastened to her neck, she struggled towards her baby to try to snatch it from the claws of the grey monsters. She could not even get near the cradle. There were too many cats for her to fight alone. In despair she ran to the window, flung it open and screamed into the empty night. "Help!"

Yet another cat jumped into the room, this time as black as the night it came from. No one else heard her desperate cry.

Now something extraordinary was happening. The cat on

Jane's shoulder dropped to the floor. The other cats, who had been teasing and biting the children in their beds sprang to the ground. The centre of the room became a seething, snarling mass of fur. Jane watched, horrified but relieved. She saw the black cat tear itself away from the struggle. It shot out of the room, the others pursuing it like a pack of hounds.

ALEXANDER FRAZER had felt uneasy about William leaving his family again. Although he would not admit that he had changed his mind about witchcraft, he was sure that Jane's cats were more than a dream, and he thought that they would strike again. The next day he decided to call at the Montgomery's house first.

He knocked; twice, three times. Of course, the family might well be out. They would not expect him so early. Yet Frazer was even more anxious. He tried the handle of the door; it was locked. He looked for an open window. There was one upstairs. He was just able to reach it by climbing on to the porch.

It was the window of the children's bedroom. He peered in, and for a moment he thought they were all four dead. The baby's head was bleeding; the boys both had blood on their faces; a long trickle of blood was seeping down Jane's neck. He stood transfixed by the awful sight. Then the baby began to whimper.

Frazer crept over to the cradle. He bent over the child, who started to cry in earnest at the sight of the stranger's face. The mournful yelling raised his hopes. If the baby had been seriously hurt, it would never have managed to make such a noise. He turned to Jane and the other two children. They were alive as well.

He fetched some water to bathe their wounds. He was relieved to find that none of them was very deep. He was not surprised to find that they looked like the marks of claws and teeth.

This time Frazer sent a messenger from the inn to fetch William Montgomery. He was determined to remain in the neighbourhood, in order to be at the cottage from the moment dusk began to fall. He also wanted to make a small investigation. He therefore made one more rent-collecting call that morning—to Margaret Nin-Gilbert.

Margaret was a long time coming to the door. Her arm was bandaged. Her face was covered in scratches and bites —like Jane's, only larger and deeper. She smiled painfully as she handed over the rent. Frazer thanked her curtly. His suspicions were confirmed. Tonight he intended to get proof that she was plaguing the Montgomerys. Then he would show no mercy. He would report her to the sheriff.

MARGARET WAS determined to go to the Montgomery's that night. She had to do what she could for Jane and the children.

Madge Olson was also determined to be there. She had tasted human blood. Her fun and revenge were not going to be spoiled by anyone, least of all by Margaret Nin-Gilbert. She and her friends were more than a match for Margaret. They would scratch her to death if necessary. It was to be a real party at the Montgomery's house tonight.

Had either of them known that Frazer would be waiting for them, and that William Montgomery was already riding furiously to join him, they would have stayed away.

When he got home, William found Frazer sitting downstairs alone. Jane had felt too unwell to wait up. The two men sat in silence, starting at every tiny noise. Fraser's hand was poised on his pistol. William was clutching his sword.

"How do they get in?" whispered William.

"They just appear." Frazer shuddered. He could do with some whisky. He went across to his bag and bent down to open it. William would surely like some too.

"Would you like a dram . . ." His sentence was cut short by a terrified scream from upstairs. Jane came rushing out of her bedroom. A grey cat was clinging to her shoulders, sinking its teeth into her neck.

In a flash the two men were at the top of the stairs. William seized the cat by its hind legs, wrenched it from his wife's neck, and hurled it over the banisters. Frazer ran straight into the children's bedroom; he was met by a mass of green eyes, glaring through the darkness. He stopped abruptly, paralyzed under the awful stare. Then the cats began to move in on him; they threw themselves at him, shrieking with satanic laughter. The sudden attack brought back his power of movement. He drew his gun; but a searing pain went through his wrist, and the gun fell to the floor. The cat who had latched on to his wrist did not let go. He tried to shake it off, but he was besieged by cats on all sides, spitting, howling, scratching and biting. He could do nothing. A cat bit into the back of his leg, making him stagger with shock and pain. Before he had regained his balance another slipped between his ankles. He felt himself falling. The next moment the cats were upon him, smothering him with their horrible furry bodies. He gasped for breath. Fur stopped his mouth and nose, then everything went black.

Jane had also fainted; William remained with her just long enough to make sure she was still alive before following Frazer into the bedroom. He found a seething mass of cats tearing at something on the floor. His children were sitting up in bed, ashen and motionless. He took a step towards Andrew and said his name softly; the boy said nothing, his eyes stared glassily, like a dead man's eyes. William reached out and touched his cheek. Suddenly, as if triggered off by a vital nerve, the boy leapt out of bed and flung himself upon the pile of cats. His father tried to drag him back. It was then that William saw Frazer's foot, the only part of his body not hidden by the cats. William raised his sword and began hacking wildly at the arched grey backs. The cats tumbled in panic away from Frazer's body. A moment later they were all gone—all, that is, except three, who lay dead on the floor.

And a fourth, whom William found sitting beside his wife at the top of the stairs.

William did not quite understand about that fourth cat. It was not the one that he had seen attacking Jane. That cat had been grey, like the rest. This one was black. Moreover, it was neither scratching nor biting, but gently licking Jane's wounds. But William did not stop to consider. He was waging a war with the witch-cats, and this was one of the enemy. It backed away hissing as William pointed his sword. As soon as it was far enough away from Jane, William swiped at it. The cat turned and fled. As it ran down the stairs, William noticed to his great satisfaction that its leg was bleeding.

THE NEXT day the inn was all of a buzz. Three women in the town had died suddenly and mysteriously. Several others were lame or wearing slings. There had been strange goings on at William Montgomery's cottage, and Mr Frazer had been seriously hurt.

"Serves him right," one of the fishermen was saying. "He wouldn't take notice of our warnings. He laughed at . . ." The fisherman's voice tailed off. Frazer was standing in the door, supported by William Montgomery. He was breathing very heavily and his face and hands were covered in deep red scratches.

"I owe you all an apology," he said hoarsely," so I came to buy you a drink." William helped him to a chair. The men stared at him with horror. This was the first time that they had seen their tales of witchcraft come so brutally true.

Just then another fisherman joined them, agog with yet another sensational piece of news. "Her leg's dropped off!" The newcomer looked round for some reaction, but the company was still stunned by Frazer's appearance. "I said her leg's dropped off—on her doorstep," he added dramatically. Still no one took any notice. The man became desperate. "Margaret Nin-Gilbert's . . ." he began again.

The effect was electric. William shot across the room and clutched him violently by the shoulder. Frazer rose unsteadily to his feet and started to yell excitedly, "Tell us man! Tell us! Tell us!"

The fisherman shrank away nervously. Mr Frazer seemed to be in a very strange mood. Nevertheless he had seen it, with his own eyes. He plucked up courage; "All black it was," he stammered, "I saw it on her doorstep—just fell off as if someone had cut it—Margaret Nin-Gilbert's leg."

Frazer thanked him, then he and William left the inn. One of the cats had been identified, the black cat that William had wounded in the leg. Frazer could no longer doubt that Margaret Nin-Gilbert was one of the cat-witches.

Sick as he was, he was going to see the sheriff of Caithness.

THE NEXT day the constable came for Margaret Nin-Gilbert. She accepted her arrest meekly. She admitted she was guilty. She had given herself to the Devil many years ago. She had tried to put a harmful spell on Mr Frazer, which had not succeeded. She had been forced into this by her master the Devil, and by Madge Olson. She had been in William Montgomery's house in the form of a cat, and had been wounded in the leg by William himself. Madge Olson and several other women, who were also witches, had been there at the same time. Margaret knew that it was no good trying to explain that she and Madge had become deadly enemies, that she had only wished to help Jane and her children.

On her testimony Madge Olson was also arrested. She did not seem to care. She was intoxicated with witchcraft. She was not afraid to burn.

Frazer paid them both a visit in prison as soon as he was well enough. He was hailed by everyone as a hero, a defender of right; but he was still not quite happy about the outcome of his detective work. He wanted to talk to the two women just once more.

His interview with Madge Olson was short.

"I came to see if I could bring you any help or comfort," he said. Madge's green eyes glittered mockingly.

"It must be nice to be somebody," she retorted. "If you don't want your tenants any more, just have them burned." She began to laugh at his scarred face. "But you'll always have my marks on your face. You'll never be able to forget me."

Margaret Nin-Gilbert received him with her usual politeness, although she could only raise herself slightly from her straw bed to greet him. She looked grey and very fragile. When he asked her if she needed anything she smiled gratefully but shook her head. Frazer felt a sudden urge to try and save her from her misery. He knew now what did not fit. This woman was not evil like the other. She could not have plagued Jane and her children, because there was something inside her that was good and kind.

"I know you've been wrongly accused," he said. "I know that I myself have misjudged you, but I don't know how. Please tell me." Margaret's eyes brightened with a glimmer of hope.

"I'll explain to the sheriff. I won't let them burn you," Frazer went on desperately.

Margaret raised herself on her elbow. "I never harmed Mrs Montgomery or her children," she whispered. "I tried to save . . ." She never finished the sentence. She was staring straight past Frazer. He recognized the look on her face. He had seen it before, that night when he had caught sight of the black horse. He looked quickly over his shoulder. He saw nothing. When he turned back Margaret had slumped down on to her bed. She was dead.

4

The Monk's Devil

Brother Michel sat in a shadowy corner of the chapel, watching. He had been doing so for months now, and had seen the sculptors turn the inert wall of stone into a mass of figures so vivid that they were almost alive. At the top, saints and angels prayed and played harps; while hideous demons tormented writhing sinners in the inferno below.

At first watching was enough; but gradually Brother Michel began to long to join them in their creation. He had never handled a chisel, or any tool that needed much skill; he was only the keeper of the treasure vault below the chapel; but he felt sure that he could do it.

Confidently he approached the sculptors' foreman, and asked, "Would you like some help?"

The foreman looked at him in amazement. "What sort of help?"

"Mine. I should like to carve something."

There was a burst of laughter from the sculptors. The idea! An upstart monk who thought he could do their trade without any training!

"What's the matter?" asked Michel, indignant at their laughter.

The men only laughed more.

"You just try. You'll soon find out," said the foreman, handing Michel his chisel and sitting down and folding his arms mockingly.

Brother Michel took the tool angrily. Let them mock! he thought. He would show them! He began chipping away furiously at the stone.

Perhaps it was his bad temper that made him choose to carve a devil, not an angel. Perhaps it was the same black humour that guided his hand to create something so horrifying and gruesome. Or perhaps, as Michel came to believe, he had been inspired by God.

One by one the sculptors put down their own tools and began to watch Michel. Their first amusement soon turned to surprise at the sureness of his hands; then, as the face of the Devil began to take shape, they trembled with fear. This face was more ghastly and more hideously evil than anything they had ever seen in their lives before. Its mouth was like an open sore; its fangs like murderous daggers; most terrible of all were its eyes, forcing the men to turn away in pain and terror. It made their own grotesque carvings seem at most minor devils toying with sin. It was surely the face of Satan himself.

Michel's fellow monks were even more overcome. Here was a Devil that portrayed evil in its full horror. Anyone who saw it would know at once what evil was. So the Abbot announced that the chapel should be open to the public every day, in order that as many people as possible should see the carving and be driven away from sin by it. Soon The Monk's Devil became famous. Everyone was delighted.

Everyone, that is, except Satan.

Satan was very upset by the ugliness of the carving. He was a thousand times more upset when he discovered that people were coming to the monastery from far and wide to see it, and that The Monk's Devil was a byword that made everyone who heard it shudder and grimace. He could not bear people to believe he was so hideous. He had to put things right. He decided to pay Michel a visit.

MATINS, THE prayers held at midnight to greet the new day, had just finished. The monks could rest until daybreak. Michel walked back towards his cell through the echoing cloisters. He was tired but happy. Crowds had again been filing through the chapel to see his sculpture. He had watched them all day approach it, then turn their eyes away in horror, their faces pallid from the shock of what they saw. He was certain now that he had been inspired by God to carve this portrait, and he was proud to have been chosen. He opened the door of his cell.

The small, bare room felt unusually warm and stuffy. A soft red glow filtered through the dark. Michel peered around him. At first he could see nothing, but his eyes grew slowly used to the dim light. Suddenly he gave a sharp cry. There was a figure leaning against the far wall.

"Good evening," said the figure politely.

"What are you doing here?" shrieked the monk. "Who are you?"

"Don't you recognize me?"

"No!"

"I thought you might not," replied the figure, "your portrait of me was so very inexact."

Then Michel knew whom he was speaking to. He backed away fearfully.

"There is nothing to be afraid of," said Satan. "As you can see, I am much less horrific than you thought."

Michel had to admit that this was true. He would rather look at the real Satan than his portrait any day.

"That is why I am here," went on the Devil. "I've come to ask you to smash up your carving of me and start again. I'll even sit for you if you like," he added helpfully.

The monk was aghast. His sculpture was a famous masterpiece, inspired by God. To destroy it would be to fly in the face of His will. He stared at the Devil with fearful eyes. Did he dare oppose him?

Yet the Devil did not seem so terrifying, and had put his point of view most civilly. Perhaps he would not mind if Michel refused with equal politeness. Michel plucked up his courage.

"I'm afraid I can't do that," he said nervously.

The cell became uncomfortably hot; the red glow brightened; a strange hissing came from the figure by the wall. Michel trembled; he regretted his courage.

But a moment later all was cool and quiet again. Satan did not want to lose his temper. He had much better weapons. With a little patience, he could play havoc with Michel's life, corrupt his soul *and* get him to destroy the disagreeable carving.

"I'm very sorry that you could not see your way to helping me," said Satan with extreme politeness, "but I hope to have the pleasure of meeting you again soon."

Michel only wanted the Devil to go away and leave him alone.

"Goodbye," he said. But he was speaking to an empty room.

Had it all been a dream, brought on by the excitement over the sculpture? Whatever it was, he preferred to blot the memory from his mind.

HAD IT been a dream?

Not far away, not long afterwards, Jeanne de Crecy, lying on her hard bed, was asking herself the same question. The cold room had become warm. She remembered a soft red glow. Someone had been there with her, but she had not seen who it was. Someone had spoken to her.

"Look The Monk's Devil in the eye. Do that without fear and you will find love and riches." The words still echoed in her ears.

Jeanne was lonely and poor. More than anything else in the world she wanted love and riches. Even if it had been a dream, she had nothing to lose by obeying the mysterious speaker, she thought. She had heard talk of the famous Monk's Devil; how hideous it was, how no one could bear to glance at it for more than a second. But she felt sure she could look it in the eye. Jeanne was suddenly determined. She jumped out of bed, pulled on her threadbare dress and set out for the monastery.

When she came into the chapel, Jeanne made straight for the sculpture of the Devil. Like everybody else she stopped and reeled away, pale with horror; but she did not stay back. Instead she braced herself to look at it again. This time her eyes stayed trained on it for a moment before she looked away. Again and again she forced herself to look at the carving, even though she felt utterly repelled by it.

From his shadowy corner of the chapel, Michel watched

her amazed. Never before had anyone stared at his sculpture so long and so boldly.

She came back again the next day, and the next, and the next, determined to learn to keep her gaze fixed upon the carving. Michel found himself wondering about her. Why did she have to look at his carving like this? Who was she? He thought about her more and more, even when he was at prayer. Finally he could no longer resist the temptation to speak to her.

"Do you *like* my sculpture?"

Jeanne looked The Monk's Devil in the eye. The eye promised her love and riches. She turned to Michel and nodded.

After that Michel and Jeanne often spoke in the chapel. Michel learned that her father had been killed fighting the English, leaving her alone and so poor that she did not have enough to eat. Michel felt sad and angry; the monks, although they had all sworn themselves to poverty, always had well-filled bellies. Why should Jeanne go hungry? The sight of ample dinners on the refectory table began to tempt him: one evening he slipped some bread and meat from the table unnoticed into his wide sleeves. The following day, in the chapel, he gave it to Jeanne.

"Thou shalt not steal!" He had broken one of God's Ten Commandments.

From now on, Michel stole bread and meat every day for Jeanne. At first he was guilty and nervous, but gradually he began to enjoy the excitement of stealing. Soon he stopped passing the food to her in the chapel, where they might easily be seen. Instead they met outside the monastery, in the secrecy of the night.

For a monk pledged to a life without women, this was a

greater sin than stealing food. But Michel did not care any more. Monastery laws meant nothing compared with Jeanne.

It annoyed Michel to see her threadbare clothes, while in a vault beneath the chapel lay the treasure of which he was keeper, unseen and useless. One jewel from that treasure would buy a host of beautiful dresses.

The key to the vault hung heavily on Michel's belt. "Thou shalt not steal!" Why not?

MATINS WERE OVER. Slowly the monks filed out of the chapel, to sleep or to pray in their cells. Michel stayed in the chapel alone, pretending to be deeply absorbed in prayer. When all was silent he stood up and crept across to the door that led to the treasure vault. Fumblingly he put the key in the lock and turned it. The door swung open with a long creaking groan. Michel held his breath. Had anyone heard him? But there was no sound in the chapel.

Beyond the door was a flight of steps; Michel walked down them gingerly, every step ringing out through the darkness like a summons. There was not even a chink of light in the underground room, but Michel knew exactly where the treasure was. He reached out and grabbed the first object that came to hand. Then, his heart pounding, he raced back up the steps. He locked the door behind him. He was safe. He knelt down in the chapel and waited till his heartbeat grew quiet.

When he got back to his cell Michel saw what he had stolen. It was the Cross of Sainte Mathilde, made of priceless jewels.

Jeanne's face shone with delight when Michel gave her the crucifix. Now she knew for certain that the mysterious stranger's words were coming true. Michel had brought her riches, and he could only have stolen from his own monastery for one reason: he must love her.

When Michel returned to the monastery after his meeting with Jeanne, he discovered that the Abbot wanted to see him. Surely no one could have found him out? His mouth felt dry with fear as he entered the Abbot's cell.

"The Cross of Sainte Mathilde has disappeared!"

"That is not possible!" Michel put on a face of wide-eyed amazement.

"It has happened," said the Abbot sharply, "and you are to blame!"

Michel's heart missed a beat. He *had* been found out!

"You are responsible for keeping the vault locked. Nobody else, apart from myself, has a key. If someone has entered it is by your carelessness! Did you leave the key anywhere last night?"

If he confessed to this, thought Michel, then he would not be suspected of theft.

"I'm afraid I left it on my table all night," he replied, "while I was asleep."

The Abbot turned pale.

"You are not responsible," he gasped angrily. "You have lost all sense of duty to the monastery. That is a sin, my son!"

Michel listened to the Abbot in silence.

"Give me the key to the treasure vault! You are not fit to be keeper of our treasure!"

Michel handed over the key without a word. The Abbot took it and hung it on his own belt. Then Michel left the room, seething with indignation at the way the Abbot had treated him, and quite forgetting that he deserved far worse.

The evening passed uncomfortably for Michel. The other monks kept glancing at him with contempt; he even thought he saw a trace of suspicion in the eyes of some of them. One in particular, Brother Jacques, looked at him as though he was trying to see into his thoughts. The next day was no better. No-one would talk to him or return his smiles. Even the sight of the stream of visitors coming in to see his sculpture did not cheer him. The only thing that gave him happiness was the thought of his evening meeting with Jeanne.

Jeanne had spent her day very happily, dreaming. She was very near to having what she wanted more than anything else in the world: love and riches. Her only regret was that the man who loved her was a monk and could not marry her. In her dream he proved his love for her by leaving the monastery and running away with her. In her dream they lived happily ever after on the money they got for the precious stones of the crucifix. Why shouldn't the dream come true? At least, she thought, there could be no harm in saying something to Michel about it.

"I'll leave with you tonight!" cried Michel when she told him. He had had quite enough of the monastery. Life with Jeanne was far more attractive. They arranged that Jeanne should wait for Michel outside the north door of the chapel. He would join her straightaway after Matins.

But a second plan was beginning to take shape in Michel's mind which Jeanne did not know about; it was a plan that would pay the Abbot and his monks out for their ill-treatment of him, and one which would make Michel and Jeanne very rich indeed.

That night, Michel returned quickly to his cell after Matins. He stood listening at his door till the monks had all padded their ways to their cells. Then he crept out into the dark stone corridor. Here and there a glow shone beneath the door of a cell, where a monk was still praying or reading by the light of a candle. The Abbot's cell was in darkness. Michel listened for a moment at the door. He could hear regular heavy breathing. The Abbot was asleep. Very carefully he opened the door. He could just see the bulky shape of the old monk lying on his mattress. Michel crept across to the mattress and bent down over the old monk. With trembling fingers he began to untie the belt around the Abbot's waist, trying not to touch his body. The Abbot stirred, making Michel crouch back into the darkest shadow. But he did not wake. Michel returned to his task.

After what seemed like an eternity, the knot came free. Joyously Michel slid his prize off the belt. It was the confiscated key to the treasure vault.

Michel thought the chapel would be empty, but he was wrong. A lone monk was kneeling before the altar. Shaking with impatience, Michel knelt down at the back of the chapel. Suppose the monk were to stay there all night? Suppose Jeanne were to think he wasn't coming? What if the Abbot woke and found the key missing?

At last the monk got up and walked slowly back down the centre aisle of the chapel. It was Brother Jacques. The monk turned and went into the main buildings of the monastery. He did not seem to notice Michel.

As soon as he could no longer hear the monk's footsteps, Michel hurried to open the door of the treasure vault. This time he did not trouble about the noise. The important thing was speed. He whipped a sack from beneath his robe as he ran down the stone steps. As soon as he was at the bottom he began shoving the priceless treasure of the monastery pell mell into the sack. He took everything, from bishops' coronets to saints' bones. There was no time to sort out what was valuable and what was useless. The saints' relics he could toss away later. Then he raced back up the stairs and into the chapel, leaving the door wide open behind him, ran past his stone carving of Satan, and flung open the north door. Jeanne and freedom awaited him outside.

Footsteps echoed on the stone floor of the chapel. Jeanne screamed. Hands seized him roughly, and he found himself looking into the eyes of Brother Jacques.

Michel was taken by the monks to another vault below the chapel, and chained to the wall. There they left him. Water was seeping through the stone and down his back, but he could not move more than an inch away from it. Even that made the chains cut into his wrists and ankles. Michel was shivering feverishly, partly with the cold, partly with fear. His teeth would not stop chattering. Did the monks intend just to leave him to rot down here? Or would he be sent to burn at the hands of some ruthless church court?

Suddenly the air grew warmer. The darkness gave way to a red glow. Satan was standing right beside him.

The Devil was feeling very pleased with himself. With very little effort, just a few words in Jeanne's ear, he had managed to set these two frail human beings on exactly the course to disaster that he wanted. He was sure that he would have no trouble now in persuading Michel to destroy that hideous sculpture.

"So we *do* meet again," he said jauntily.

Michel felt almost pleased to see him. Nothing could be worse than the cold, lonely anguish of a moment before.

JANE EDMONDS

"Actually," went on the Devil, "I came to see if I could be of any help to you."

"The only help I need is someone to get me out of here," said Michel bitterly.

"My thought exactly," replied Satan. "But you need a little help in proving your innocence once you're out, don't you? Otherwise they'll just chain you up again."

"But I'm not innocent!" cried Michel, tears starting from his eyes. "And everybody knows it! I was caught red-handed!"

"Never mind about that," said the Devil. "I can set you free and convince the whole monastery that you are innocent."

Michel stared at him in disbelief.

"How?"

"By pretending that you were me. If I set you free from those chains and shackle myself in your place, the monks will think that the person they caught with their treasure was really *me* disguised as *you*. All *you* have to do is to go quietly back to your cell and pretend you haven't left it all night."

Michel brightened.

"Would you really do that for me?"

"No!" Satan watched Michel's face fall. He smiled to himself. Now was the moment to play his trump card. "Not unless you smash up your stone carving of me."

"I will do it as soon as I am free!" cried Michel without a moment's hesitation.

"And you will carve a handsome portrait in its place?"

"I will make you look as beautiful as any angel!" pleaded Michel.

As soon as he had said this, Michel's arms felt light. He

was no longer weighed down by chains. He was standing free in the very spot that the Devil had occupied a moment ago. Next to him, Satan, pinned down by the heavy shackles, leaned against the damp wall.

"Off you go," said the Devil, "it will ruin everything if they find you here."

Michel went.

The monks were very puzzled when they saw Michel emerge from his cell for early morning service. An accusing crowd quickly gathered round him.

"How did you get free?"

"Free from what?" asked Michel innocently.

"We put you in chains! You stole the treasure!"

"What treasure?" said Michel with a puzzled frown.

"You were caught, with a woman!"

"A woman?" Michel forced Jeanne's image from his mind. He could not be blamed. Even Saint Pierre had denied all knowledge of Jesus Christ when in fear of death.

"What woman?" he said.

The monks were astonished. Michel seemed not to know about either his crime or his punishment; and yet they had seen him, making his escape from the chapel with the treasure in his hands. Their eyes and ears must be fooling them. They spoke together, and decided to inspect the damp vault where they had chained Michel.

The vault was curiously warm. It glowed a dim red. A manacled figure was leaning against the wall, just where they had left Michel the night before. In the obscure glow it looked exactly like the monk. Brother Jacques stepped forward to look closely. The other monks heard him gasp. They saw him make the sign of the Cross.

"Father protect me!" he cried.

The figure in chains laughed. The red glow became brighter and hotter. They could see now that the figure was that of the Devil. All together the monks fell on their knees, screaming and praying.

"By the sign of Jesus Christ, go! In the name of our Father, do not touch us! In the name of the Son! In the name of our Lord! For the sake of the Holy Ghost!" The words came tumbling out in breathless panic.

Satan leant against the damp wall, enjoying their confusion. This was a special treat, apart from his success with Michel. When he got bored, he left.

The vault felt suddenly cold. The glow was gone. The chains hung limp. The Devil had disappeared. One by one the monks rose from their knees and went to seek their brother Michel's forgiveness for the wrong they had done him.

The next day The Monk's Devil was found smashed into a thousand pieces.

5
The Victim

KARL STOOD at the bottom of the great chasm, alone, listening nervously. It was a sombre, starless night, but the snow-capped mountains still gleamed dimly. The vast black rocks lowered, threatening. The world was a bleak place up here, where man and beast rarely ventured, but where Karl was obliged to wait every night. Often Karl thought that death would be better than the slavery he now endured. Yet now that his life was once again threatened, he realized he would suffer anything just to go on living.

At any moment he might hear him coming—his master, who had decided that it was time for him to die.

Three years ago his master had saved his life: on the eve of Karl's execution he had appeared in his cell. He had opened the door and led him out of the courthouse past the sleeping guards. He had lifted him on to his great black horse, and ridden with him up into the mountains, where his gaolers could not find him.

Karl had never understood how he had come to kill Liese. He had loved her. He and some friends had been practising spear-throwing in the meadow, and Liese had been teasing him because his spear always fell shorter than any of the others. He had walked away, hurt and miserable. He had met a stranger, a fair-haired young man, who had given him his own spear. The stranger had told him that it would fly higher and farther than all the rest. Karl had run back eagerly to his friends. He still remembered their mocking laughter as he cried, "Look! I can beat you all!"

He still remembered Liese running across the meadow calling to him, "If you throw it this far, I'll marry you!"

The sound of her scream as the spear struck her still rang in his ears.

In return for saving him from execution, Karl had served his master faithfully. But this, it seemed, was no longer enough.

Sick with fear, he waited, his heart thudding painfully. He had one brittle hope only, to which he clung, like a squirrel to a dead twig. He had thought of a plan to change his master's mind. If only his master would accept it!

Pounding hoves drowned Karl's heavy heartbeat. A black horse was galloping towards him across the valley. On its back, his black eyes gleaming in the night, towered the gaunt, menacing figure of his master, Satan.

The horse came to an abrupt halt. The rider grinned down at Karl.

"Are you ready?"

Karl shuddered. "Please! No! Not yet!" He blurted out his plan. "I can find you somebody else!"

Human beings were all the same, thought Satan. He never needed to seek out his own victims. They sought out each other.

Karl gazed at him in rigid suspense. What was his master

thinking? Would he accept his plan to find someone to die in his place?

"Very well, find another man," said Satan, grinning. "If you succeed, you may live for another three years."

Karl gasped with relief and gratitude.

In three years he would be dead anyway, reflected Satan. It was not long to wait. In the meantime, the fool would furnish him with an additional soul. He turned his horse and galloped away through the chasm, disappearing behind the great hulk of the mountain.

As soon as he had gone, Karl hurried away in the opposite direction, leaving the chasm by a narrow, perilous ledge. Then he began scrambling downwards to more hospitable country, where men could live and work contentedly.

The lower slopes of the mountain were covered in forest. Although the woods were dense, they were not cold and cruel like the rocks higher up. At times they were broken by sunny plains and bright little villages, clustered round painted churches—like the village Karl had once lived in. Down here Karl hoped to find a victim for Satan.

The morning was warm and still as Karl made his way towards the first village. The trees were sparse here. Through them Karl could see a group of men, talking and laughing. From time to time he heard a gun crack. As he got nearer he saw that they were having a friendly contest, taking it in turns to shoot down some pigeons which kept flying out from the trees. The men were mostly peasants, but two of them were dressed in the green uniform of the forester. It was the turn of one of the foresters, a fair, nervous-looking young man. A pigeon flew out of its tree; the forester fired; the pigeon flew on undisturbed. The bullet had gone nowhere near it. The other men roared with laughter.

"You won't win the Chief Forester's daughter like that!" they joked.

The young forester was not nearly so amused. He looked more nervous than ever. He walked dismally away from the group.

Karl followed him, walking briskly to catch up.

"Fine morning," he said to start the conversation.

"Mm," the young forester replied without enthusiasm.

"You don't seem too happy."

The forester turned and looked at Karl. There were tears in his eyes.

"Why don't you tell me all about it?" said Karl, looking very sympathetic.

Karl learned that the young man's name was Georg. The remark he had overheard about winning the Chief Forester's daughter was no mere joke. Georg was deeply in love with Maria and she with him. He wanted to marry her. But the Chief Forester had no sons; therefore his daughter's husband would in time succeed him. So he insisted that the chosen man should be a skilful shot. With this in mind he had set a shooting contest that was to take place in two days' time. The winner would marry Maria. Georg had never been a skilful shot. Now he seemed to get worse and worse. Everybody was laughing at him. The Chief Forester regarded him with such scorn that he would not even allow him to see his daughter. Maria was in despair. It was all hopeless.

"Not necessarily," said Karl encouragingly. "I could help you." His soft brown eyes fixed Georg eagerly.

"How?" Georg looked at him in wonder and disbelief. "You'll never be able to teach me to shoot well. Nobody could. I've tried hard for so long."

Karl felt quite sorry for him, but he pressed on with his scheme.

"I didn't say I would teach you how to shoot. But I can help you win the contest."

"It isn't possible!"

"Yes, it is," replied Karl confidently, adding gently, "if you will put your trust entirely in me."

Georg eyed the stranger. He must have been very handsome once, with his huge brown eyes and dark curly hair; he was still young, but deep lines of suffering had destroyed his looks. It was the face of a man who had seen much and knew much. Georg thought that he could trust him.

"I will," he said.

At that moment there was a rustling in the trees and the sound of hooves on soft pine needles. A shadow blocked the sun, making the air suddenly chilly. The two men looked up, startled. A huntsman in a deerskin jerkin was gazing down at them from a great black horse. The huntsman winked one of his glittering black eyes at Karl; then turned his horse and rode away.

"Who was that?" asked Georg, puzzled.

"Just an acquaintance of mine," replied Karl casually.

That night, high up in the mountains, hidden in his secret chasm, Satan moulded a bullet. He gave the bullet to Karl, who loaded his gun with it. Then Karl returned to the forest to seek out Georg.

Georg was happy for the first time for several weeks. He had had no hope of winning the contest. Now it seemed possible. The curly-haired stranger appeared so confident. Georg was longing to tell Maria the good news. Early next morning he made his way furtively to her house, expecting the Chief Forester to jump out on him at any moment. With pounding heart, he threw a fir cone at Maria's window in the high sloping roof.

The window opened. When Maria saw Georg, she looked alarmed.

"I've got to talk to you," said Georg urgently. "Can you get out?"

"Father's downstairs!"

"I know, but I've got some wonderful news. Please try."

"I'll see if I can creep out without disturbing him." Maria took off her shoes and tiptoed out of the room and down the stairs, clinging to the bannister for fear of stumbling and alerting her father. A minute later she was running through the grass towards Georg.

"I'm going to win the contest tomorrow," he told her.

Maria stopped short, amazed by Georg's sudden confidence. For months he had been saying that it was hopeless. Was this his wonderful news?

"You seem very sure. Has your shooting improved?" she asked him doubtfully.

"Not a jot! But I have met a man who will help me to win!"

Maria felt angry with Georg for being so stupid. "It isn't possible," she said dourly.

"It is, I swear it," replied Georg. "You would understand if you had spoken to him."

Maria's eyes filled with tears. "How can you be so silly! He's playing a trick on you!" Unable to bear his crazy stupidity, she turned on her heels and ran off into the woods, weeping uncontrollably.

"He can't be playing a trick!" cried Georg, setting off after her. His heart, which had been so full of hope, was heavy with doubts now. Perhaps she was right. He probably had been a fool.

"Georg!" Karl was coming towards him through the trees. "I have something to show you."

"I'm busy," called Georg, wondering what had happened to Maria.

"It will help you to win your contest."

Maria's anger and disbelief had almost convinced Georg that the man was a fraud. Yet Karl's words arrested him. They seemed straightforward and honest. Besides, Georg wanted to believe them. He had no other hope of winning the contest.

"Let me see," he said, deliberately putting aside his mistrust.

Karl held out his gun, smiling. For a moment he had been in danger of losing Georg. He would feel safer once Georg had fired the gun that contained Satan's bullet.

"I want you to try this," he said. Georg took the gun.

"Will it help me to shoot straight?" he questioned wryly.

"Try it and see!"

"What shall I aim for?" asked Georg. He did not expect much of the gun, but he did feel a faint thrill of hope. Suppose he did by some strange chance hit his target?

Karl pointed upwards between the tall trees. High above in the blue sky they could just glimpse an eagle circling.

"Aim for the eagle," he said. Georg's hope vanished.

"It's impossible!"

"Just shoot."

George shrugged. He did not aim carefully. There was no point. The eagle was too high up, too difficult to sight.

The bullet screamed through the air. The eagle fell like a stone at his feet. Karl grinned.

"If you shoot like that tomorrow you will win Maria."

"If!" It would be too good to be true, thought Georg. Karl decided to risk telling him more.

"The bullet you fired from my gun was a charmed bullet. It goes exactly where you will it to go."

It took Georg a few moments to take in what Karl had said. It was so unexpected. Georg felt suddenly uneasy. How did Karl come by the bullet? Surely such bullets were got only by sorcery.

"I can provide you with enough of those bullets to win the contest," Karl went on.

Enchanted bullets? Bullets, Georg knew in his heart, that ordinary god-fearing men should not meddle with.

"And to win Maria!" insisted Karl, disturbed by Georg's thoughtful silence.

What did it matter if the bullets were enchanted? Maria was what mattered, thought Georg, and with the help of those bullets he would be able to marry her. He did not care if they were evil or dangerous. He would be turning them to good purpose.

"I will need seven for the contest," he said at last.

"By all means," said Karl, relieved, "but you will have to help me a little."

"I'll do anything," said Georg. Karl felt encouraged. Georg appeared to be won over.

"I want you to come with me tonight when I go for the bullets."

"Of course," said Georg. It seemed a small request in return for the great favour Karl was doing him. "Where are we going?"

Karl pointed to a dark mountain peak that towered above the forest.

"There."

Georg felt the blood draining from his cheeks. Nobody ever went there. It was said to be a terrible place. Some even said it was haunted by the Devil.

"Surely you don't believe all that old gossip?" scoffed Karl, noticing Georg's sudden pallor.

"N-no," replied George, ashamed of his fear! but he could not refrain from asking nervously, "Does someone live up there?"

"Just an acquaintance of mine." Georg remembered the black-eyed huntsman he had seen on the previous day in the forest. Was it from him they would get the bullets? Where did he get the power to enchant them? Why did he live so high up on the grim mountain that all men were warned to avoid? How did Karl know him? The questions flooded Georg's troubled mind. Karl watched him intently; he knew he had to scotch Georg's fears.

"It would be a pity not to come. Now that you know you have the means to win the contest, you would regret it all your life if you let the chance go. Think how you will feel when you see Maria married to another man, knowing that it could have been you!"

He was right. Georg decided to forget his doubts.

"I'll see you tonight," he said, more light-heartedly than he felt.

Maria had run on into the forest too distraught to care where she was going. It was unbearable that Georg had no hope of winning the shooting contest. Now his behaviour made it worse than ever. She wished she had the sense not to love him; but she could not help herself. All she could do was run and sob.

Then she became aware of something huge blocking her

path. She looked up and saw a shining black flank. A horse was standing there, quite still. On it sat a huntsman in a deerskin jerkin. He was smiling at her. But there was something about him that made her shudder. Her sobs ceased, stifled by fear.

The huntsman slid lightly off his horse. He caught her firmly by the arm and pulled her round to look her in the face. He held her there motionless, staring at her with glinting black eyes that filled her soul with terror.

"Do you truly love the forester Georg?" he asked mockingly.

Maria nodded, afraid to speak. To her relief the huntsman let go of her arm.

"Then you'll go to his rescue when he's in danger?" The huntsman did not wait for a reply, but leapt back on to his horse and rode away laughing.

For a moment Maria stood wondering what the huntsman could mean. Then the sobs began again; fear joined her misery. Slowly she turned and made her way back home.

If Georg had managed to ignore his doubts down in the forest, he could no longer do so that night, as he followed Karl upwards towards the dark mountain peak. As they got nearer, it appeared more and more sinister and hostile. The air was bitterly cold, numbing his fingers so that he could hardly grip the jagged rocks as he scrambled across them. For a while they had been able to walk, but now the journey had become a perilous climb. Great crevasses yawned unexpectedly in the darkness, ready to swallow any man that put a foot wrong. It was an ungodly place.

Karl seemed to know his way well.

"Do you often come up here?" asked Georg. He was sure now that Karl was tampering with something forbidden and dangerous. He knew that Karl was drawing him into it. Yet surely Karl could mean him no harm? He was doing his utmost to help him.

Karl pretended not to hear the question. He was aware of Georg's rising suspicions and was terrified of saying something that would make him turn back. His master was expecting them. If he arrived in the chasm without Georg, he would have failed. His master would allow him no second chance.

"It's not much further," he said encouragingly.

The two men went on in silence. They were climbing up a massive rock face, streaked with thin sheets of treacherous black ice. One slip and they would fall hundreds of feet down into the void below. It was too dangerous to talk.

After what seemed like hours, they reached a tiny ledge, at the far end of which was a long slit in the rock. Georg gasped with relief; here, at least for a few minutes, was safety. Karl was also relieved. For this was the ledge leading to the chasm where Georg was to meet his master.

"This way," he said to Georg, and slipped through the gap in the rocks. Georg followed.

A bright light was shining, dazzling after the darkness of the night. Georg could hardly hold his eyes open at first. He seemed to be in a deep gully. Black stone towered on all sides, gleaming in the cruel light. As his eyes became more used to the glare, Georg turned his head to the spot that shone brightest of all.

The light came from a fire about half way along the gully. But it was like no fire that Georg had ever seen. The flames were not orange, but blue-white. They did not flicker and glow but cut through the darkness like blades. In the centre of the fire was a black cauldron. Behind it stood a tall, gaunt figure. All at once Georg felt more terrified even than he had felt on the heartless rock face of the mountain. Something about the weird figure bent over the cauldron was more ominous than death itself.

Karl took him by the arm. He felt cold. Georg looked at his face. It was very white. Karl was afraid too.

"Come with me," said Karl, and led him towards the fire.

"Here you are!" said Karl to his master nervously, sounding to Georg almost as if he were offering a sacrifice.

"Hold your arm over the fire!" commanded the stranger.

Georg looked at Karl, who nodded at him encouragingly. To his horror, Georg realized that the command was meant for him. Was Karl mad? Those flames would burn. He shrank away from the fire.

"Well, Karl?" There was a sharp note of menace in the stranger's voice. Karl shuddered. He must not let Georg go now.

"Don't be afraid Georg, those flames will not hurt you. They will bring you good. If you do as you're told, Maria will be yours."

"I'm afraid!"

"Does Maria mean so little?" For the first time Karl's soft voice sounded harsh.

Of course, he was right. Georg held out his arm and thrust it into the flames. Karl had been speaking the truth; he felt no pain. He should not have mistrusted him.

The stranger took his wrist, and drew his long fingernail delicately across it. A tiny cut appeared in the vein. A drop of blood fell into the cauldron, then another, then a third. After the seventh the vein bled no more and the cut vanished.

JANE EDMON

The stranger's black eyes glinted. Georg had been right to suspect that the huntsman would provide the charmed bullets. He did not look so human now, but the eyes were unmistakable. Georg also knew now who the huntsman was. He had been right about that too. But he shut the thought out of his mind. What did it matter who he was?

Satan stretched out one of his long fingers and bored it down into the rock floor of the chasm. He did this six times, making six small round holes. Then he took a long-handled ladle and poured a thick, black, boiling liquid from the cauldron into each of the holes. Immediately the rock around them crumbled away, leaving six perfect, round bullets. It all took less than a minute.

"This is what you need." Satan held the bullets out to Georg. "They will go wherever you wish."

"What about the seventh? You have made only six," Karl reminded the Devil. He was indeed a good friend, thought Georg.

Satan plunged his hand into the cauldron and scooped out some more of the boiling liquid. He held it in his fist for a moment, then opened out his palm, revealing a seventh bullet—exactly like the other six.

Or so it seemed. But Karl knew differently. That bullet was also charmed, but to go not where Georg wished, but where his master willed it. That bullet would go to Georg's own heart, whatever Georg's intended target might be. In taking Georg's life, it would save Karl's for three more years. He took the bullet from his master's hand.

"I'll take care of it for you, he told Georg.

Satan smiled to himself malevolently. For Karl knew nothing of his real plan, so like the one he had used to ensnare Karl three years ago—the plan that he always used.

He would time Maria's arrival on the scene perfectly. She would die by the bullet, an innocent victim. Georg would die later by the law—unless, like Karl, he let Satan save his life. Either way, he would be no mere innocent victim but another murderer, belonging to Satan body and soul.

Georg also smiled, for the first time that night. He now had what he needed to win Maria. His ordeal was over, and he had come through it unharmed.

By morning Georg had quite forgotten that he had ever had any fears or misgivings. It had been far easier coming down the mountain than climbing up it, and both he and Karl had been in a happy, carefree mood. He was touched that Karl should be so joyful at his good fortune, and felt angry at himself for having mistrusted him. The day that he had so long dreaded had arrived, and now, thanks to Karl, it was to be a day of happiness and triumph.

The contest was to take the form of a hunt on foot, directed by the Chief Forester himself. He would point out various animals and birds that the competitors had to try to shoot. The first man to hit seven of these living targets would be the winner. Many men from surrounding forests and villages were taking part; for the post of Chief Forester, with the charming addition of Maria as a wife, was a tempting prize.

When he saw Georg among the contestants the Chief Forester did not know whether to laugh or to curse him. How the fellow had the impertinence to enter the competition, when he was known to be the worst shot for miles around! Georg, on the other hand, beamed at him confidently. The Chief Forester even fancied that he winked at his companion, a careworn young man with curly hair whom he had not seen before. He decided to ignore Georg completely.

The hunt was about to begin. The men gathered in a clearing near to the heart of the forest, eyeing each other warily. The Chief Forester raised his hand as a signal to the men to begin yelling and beating on the trees that surrounded the clearing.

A rabbit, startled by the noise, came running out of the wood.

"There!" shouted the Chief Forester, pointing at it.

A gun cracked. The rabbit lay dead. Many of the contestants were still only just beginning to take aim.

"Who fired?" asked the Chief Forester, amazed by the speed and accuracy of the shot.

"I did," replied Georg quietly.

The Chief Forester stared at him in astonishment. Was he mocking him? He had opened his mouth to call Georg a liar, when he noticed Georg's gun. It was smoking. He turned to look at the other men. None of their guns had been used. There was no doubt that Georg was telling the truth.

"Well done," said the Chief Forester grudgingly.

George reloaded his gun. He had a great advantage over the other competitors; he never needed to take careful aim, for his will alone was enough to guide the bullet to its target. Six times he hit his prey before anyone else. The men that knew him gazed at him in disbelief, those that did not know him with admiration; the Chief Forester was smiling at him benignly now. Georg felt dizzy with joy. One more bullet and Maria would be his.

It was the bullet that Karl was looking after. Karl handed it to him.

Maria had not gone to watch the contest. Instead she lay

on her bed, weak with misery. Georg could have no hope of winning the contest, she was sure. Then something knocked against Maria's window. It was a fir cone. But surely it could not have been thrown by Georg; the shooting contest had only just begun. She raised her head from her tear-sodden pillow. A second cone hit the window. Troubled, Maria got up from her bed and went to the window.

Outside stood a man. But it was not Georg. Maria felt her throat contract. It was the huntsman, leaning casually against the flank of his black horse.

"Go away!" she gasped. The same awful fear as she had felt yesterday seemed to choke her words. She was not even sure if the huntsman could hear her.

"But I must speak to you. It concerns Georg." The huntsman spoke softly, almost in a whisper. "His life is in danger. If you truly love him, you must go to the hunt now. You must prevent him from shooting the white dove."

"I hate you," gulped Maria, "why should I believe you?"

"No reason," replied the huntsman coolly. "But you'd better hurry if you want to see him alive again." Then he mounted his horse and rode off into the forest.

Maria remained motionless at the window for a minute, staring at the spot where he had just been. Then she became anxious. Suppose there *was* something in his cruel warning? Even though he was probably lying, would it not be better just to go and see that all was well? She could always just creep away again unnoticed.

She pulled on her cloak and ran for all she was worth out of the house and into the forest. The sound of cries and banging on trees told her where the men were. She plunged through the trees towards them. She could see green and brown clad figures now, standing on the edge of a clearing. Then she heard her father's voice.

"Just one more, Georg, and you will be champion."

She paused, astonished. Georg had been successful. He had been right yesterday. She had been wrong. It did not seem possible.

"Ready, my son?" Her father's voice was friendly and gentle, quite unlike the harsh tones he had used to Georg in the past. He already seemed to regard him as her husband. Maria crept forward. She saw Georg take a bullet from a man with dark curly hair and load his gun with it. Another step and she would be in the clearing, right opposite Georg. Afraid of spoiling his aim, she waited.

A white dove fluttered out of the tree immediately in front of her.

"There!" shouted her father, "the dove!"

The huntsman's warning! Maria ran forward.

"No!" she screamed.

Karl turned and saw Maria. The girl would spoil everything unless he stopped her yelling. He ran across the clearing towards her as she cried out, "Don't shoot!"

Crack! Her warning had come too late. Georg had already pressed the trigger. The bullet soared into the air, straight towards Maria.

The dove flew away over the trees. Maria screamed. There was a dull thud.

Karl was lying on the ground, immediately in front of Maria. White as a sheet, Georg dropped his gun and ran towards him.

"Let me look at him." It was the huntsman on his black horse. He jumped down and examined Karl's limp body with care. "I'm afraid he's dead."

Sadly Georg put his arm round Maria. She was shaking all over.

"He saved my life," she said.

"He was a true friend," sighed Georg, looking down at the dead man. Satan grinned to himself at the human beings' stupidity.

"I'll see he gets the funeral he deserves," he said, lifting Karl's body lightly on to his horse. One victim instead of three! It was disappointing. But there were plenty more in the world. He could do without Georg and Maria. He climbed on to his horse behind the dead man and rode away, high up into the mountains where man and beast rarely ventured.

6

The Headless Bear

WEAK RAYS of sunlight shone through the farmhouse window, touching Margaret's anxious face. Her husband Stephen lay in bed, listening to the sound of his cowman bringing in the cows from milking. The big weatherbeaten farmer looked out of place, lying there on the rosebud-embroidered pillowslips that she had stitched for him with such care. Peter, the ginger-haired farm hand, stared at them with special scorn: fancy giving those namby-pamby things to the master, he thought. Margaret was no woman to be a farmer's wife.

Margaret could feel the tears pricking at her eyelids. Stephen had been ill for three days and she had nursed him with love and care. But now he was saying that she must go away, leaving the servant Peter to look after him.

Stephen had a slight fever; that was all. He was not in the least alarmed about it. He was as strong as an ox. But he was concerned that Margaret should not catch his illness. She was as frail as he was tough. Whenever she was ill there really was cause for alarm. So he was insisting that she go and stay with her cousin, who owned a farm near Gloucester, until the danger was over. He did not like parting from her any more than she did from him, but it was the sensible thing to do.

"I'd much rather stay with you." Margaret's gentle grey eyes were brimming with tears.

"No!" said Stephen firmly. "I want you to go now. Every minute that you stand here you are in danger of catching my fever."

He sounded so stern. Margaret did not want him to be angry with her. Miserably she agreed to do as he wished.

"I'll be up and about in a day or two," said Stephen encouragingly.

"And I'll send news of him every day," grinned Peter, trying not to laugh at the woman's silliness.

As he had foretold, the news of Stephen was good, and he was soon out of bed. It was the news of Margaret, sent back the other way, that was worrying. A day after her arrival at her cousin's house, she began to feel feverish. She went to bed and lay quietly in the dark for a day and a night. Then she started to talk. She talked and laughed and screamed and cried without cease. But not to her cousin; not even to herself. She was talking to someone or something that only she could see.

Cursing himself for not having sent her away sooner, Stephen set out straight away with the cart to fetch her home. How careless of him to give her his fever!

"She don't recognize nobody," her cousin warned him when he arrived.

She'll know me, thought Stephen. Perhaps the sight of his familiar face would bring her back to her senses.

But he was wrong. She did not even see him when he

entered her room. Instead she cried, and laughed, and talked to something that no one else could see or hear.

Stephen lifted her out of bed and carried her down to the cart. Her body was light. He felt her bones almost raw through her skin, for she had not eaten since the onset of the fever.

"God, please don't let her die," he prayed.

All the way home he listened to her babbling. His nerves were brittle with her ceaseless, nonsensical chatter. He wanted to comfort her, but at the same time he wanted to shake and hit her. He drove on, biting his lip to keep back the tears and irritation.

It was already beginning to get dark when they reached home. Stephen was greatly relieved to see the farmhouse, and drew up at the door feeling almost happy.

Then Margaret began screaming. She screamed and screamed and screamed. Stephen could bear it no longer. He raised his hand and struck her across the face.

The scream stopped. For the first time since they had left her cousin's house, Margaret was silent. Her lips closed. Her eyes went dull, as if shutters had been drawn over them. Her face was blank, like a death mask.

For a moment Stephen rejoiced. The terrible flow of crazy chatter had stopped. But almost immediately he was overcome with sudden despair. Margaret's body was leaden and lifeless now. Only her heart, beating tremulously, told him that she was still alive. Gently he carried her upstairs to their bedroom, every moment fearful lest that guttering heartbeat should stop. Although she felt burning hot, her body was covered with gooseflesh. He swathed her in blankets, then carefully parted her lips and spooned in a little brandy.

Margaret opened her eyes. The brandy appeared to be working, giving Stephen fresh hope. Then Margaret began to shake and moan like someone in a fit. She sat bolt upright, her eyes feverish with excitement, and swung her feet to the floor.

"No! You must stay in bed! You are sick!" Stephen tried to lie her down again. With sudden strength, the small frail woman thrust him away from her so that he stumbled backwards across the room. She stood up and ran for the door, shrieking, "Leave me alone! Don't touch me!"

Taking no notice of her words, Stephen flung himself in front of the door just in time to stop her opening it.

"Don't touch me!" Stephen felt the panic in her voice. The curious thing was that she did not seem to be looking at him, but at something beyond him. Stephen turned to see what it was. He saw nothing but the door and the walls of the room. But as his head was turned away, Margaret hurled herself at him, and again flung him across the room with fiendish force. She opened the door.

"No! Margaret! Don't go out! You will catch your death!" Stephen cried hopelessly.

There was a footfall on the landing and a grinning face appeared. It was Peter, curious to see what all the scuffling was about. The grin did not last. Margaret knocked him out of her way with a great blow on the chest.

Peter reeled backwards breathless. The namby-pamby woman had the strength of a giant!

However, the moment's delay gave Stephen time to recover. He lunged after Margaret and dragged her back into the room, locking the door behind them. She was safe. Stephen sank on to a stool, exhausted. But the pause lasted only a second. Margaret let out a great wolf-like howl. Then she began hammering on the door, which trembled under her tiny fists. A crack appeared in one of the panels.

Stephen knew he had no strength left to fight her single-handed. This tiny sickly wife of his was too powerful for him. He went to the door and called through it to Peter to fetch help.

The crack in the door was growing. Margaret beat against it with her whole body, flinging herself at it like a desperate animal in a trap. Stephen watched her helplessly. If only she would tire! But she did not tire. If only she would listen to him! Stephen called her name, but she did not hear. If only Peter would come back! With a splintering crack, Margaret forced her hand through the door. Another blow and it would break completely.

But she never made that final blow. Instead she drew back into the room, shaking all over.

"The bear," she screeched, "the bear with no head!"

There was hammering on the other side of the door. "Open up!"

"It ain't anything of the sort," said Stephen. "It's Peter." He unlocked the door thankfully and there was Peter with three more strong farm hands.

"It's coming for me!" shrieked Margaret, backing away from the four astonished men in the doorway, her face distorted with terror. "Don't touch me! Leave me in peace!"

Stephen put his arm round her to calm her frenzied mind. He had forgotten her strength. She took him by the wrist and jerked him down on to the floor. The farm hands stared in amazement at the sight of their master overpowered by this delicate woman. They had never seen anything like it.

"We must get her to bed!" gasped Stephen.

The men moved forward obediently, but it was almost

impossible to carry her to the bed. All the time Margaret struggled and kicked with super-human force. She clawed and bit till blood streamed down their hands and necks; she screamed without cease, piercing their eardrums till they could no longer think straight. When they finally got her on to the bed, it took the four of them to hold her there. There was fear in their eyes now. A little woman could never have such strength, even if she was mad, like this one. There was only one explanation: she was possessed by the Devil.

None of the men spoke this fearful thought. They were much too afraid. They had been taught never to mention the Devil's name and to run away at the first sign of him. The Devil meant hellfire and terrible tortures. But now here they were in the same room as a woman whose body had been taken over by the fiend. With what agonies might she infect them? Into what torments might she drag them? Nightmare visions, twisted and distorted like the evil spirits carved on the church door, began to haunt them. As the night grew blacker, so did these vile shapes of their imaginations.

Stephen knew what was in their minds.

"We could pray," he said, desperate lest terror should drive them away and leave him to battle with the fiend on his own. He fetched a candle, lit it, and put it at the bedside. Then he knelt down close to his wife's pillow.

The five men knelt in the flickering light, their lips moving fervently while their hands still held down the frenzied woman. Gradually the struggling subsided. Then Margaret lay still.

"Pray with us," whispered her husband.

Feebly she raised her hands and held her palms together.

Her lips began to move. She had heard Stephen's words! She turned her head slightly upon the pillow and smiled weakly at him. She knew him again.

Then the candle went out, as if scotched by a sudden draught. The room was pitch black, invaded by an icy cold that froze the prayers on the lips of the men kneeling by the bed.

"It's there!" Margaret screamed again.

The men could see only blackness, but they sensed something in the room that wrung their hearts and deadened their limbs with terror.

"There's nothing here at all," said Stephen, trying to sound cheerful and unafraid. "I'll light the candle again, then we can all see for ourselves." He held a taper to the candle. It flared up brightly, dazzling the men for a moment. Then the flame turned black, giving no light. Nothing but a dark ill-smelling smoke came from the candle now, teasing their noses and making their eyes smart painfully.

Then the smoke began to gather into a solid mass of blackness. Something was taking form in the thin night air. It was padding towards the bed. The men cringed away in terror. They could just make out its heavy claws and bulky body.

Margaret fell silent. Her body juddered helplessly as the thing came closer. Only Stephen acted. He grabbed the stool and brought it down heavily on the black form. It was then that he realized that it had no head.

The blow made no sound. The monster did not appear to feel it. It was intent only upon Margaret. It tore the blankets from her and struck savagely with its claw on the soles of her feet, once, twice, three times. Her body was shaking with a succession of shocks that threatened to jerk her right

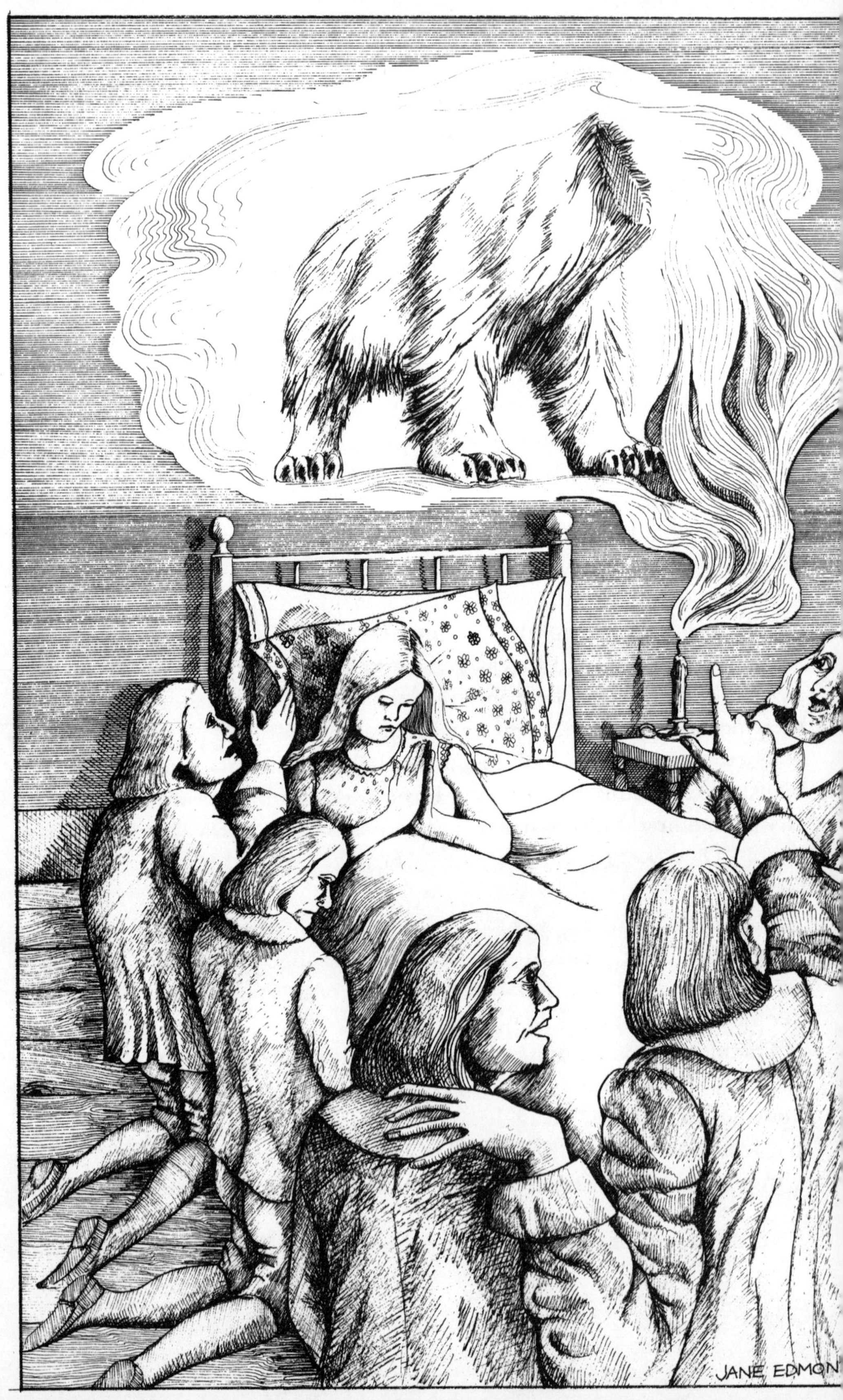
JANE EDMON

off the bed. Stephen stood petrified. He was beginning to feel numb.

The creature lifted Margaret off the bed with its great paws, and began to bat her this way and that, as if it were playing ball. Stephen watched without moving, helpless. Margaret was offering no more resistance than a dummy—a miserable bundle of cloth and flesh being tossed and batted towards the door. Stephen no longer saw her as Margaret, the wife he loved. He felt disgusted and appalled, but could not find it in him to save her any more.

The monster and its toy vanished from sight. Then the men heard something crashing down the stairs.

Several minutes went by. The men neither moved nor spoke. None of them wanted to go out of the room. It was peaceful here now, and they could not face any more horror.

As his feelings returned, Stephen began to realize the awfulness of what had happened. That empty bed was his wife's bed. She had been snatched from it by some evil thing that had beaten her down the stairs. And he, her husband, who loved and cherished her, had just looked on without lifting a finger to save her.

Panic-stricken, he rushed out of the bedroom and on to the landing. He looked down. Margaret was lying in a crumpled heap at the bottom of the stairs. Around her flickered a circle of blue-red flames, licking their way malevolently towards her. There was no sign of the headless monster.

Stephen ran down the stairs and thrust himself through the flames. Their thick bitter smell made him retch and cough, but he did not notice. Nor did he feel their rays eating into his skin, so intent was he on saving Margaret. He took her in his arms and stumbled back up the stairs, gasping for breath. Coughing and sobbing, he laid Margaret on the bed. He felt terribly sick; then he fainted.

"I HOPE Peter'll be back with the priest soon." Stephen recognized one of the farm hands speaking. Was someone dying? Everything was so blurred. He tried desperately to drag himself back to life. Suddenly he remembered Margaret.

"No bones broken." The men were saying. "A miracle! I thought she were dead!"

So Margaret was not badly hurt, and certainly not dying. So why was the priest coming?

"How did he get them burns? He looks like he's been through hell-fire itself!"

Stephen could feel the burns all right. They gnawed deep into his flesh, tormenting him. Of course! He remembered clearly now: his wife's strange fits, the headless monster, the blue-red flames. They must all be forms of the Devil who was trying to possess Margaret. Well, he could hardly be expected to come out of an encounter with the Devil unscathed. But surely he wasn't dying? He didn't need a priest.

Then the thought struck him. Perhaps those foolish men were sending for the priest to exorcise the Devil—when he, Stephen, had got rid of it already! Did they not realize that his victory over the fiend made the priest unnecessary?

"We don't need the priest," he said.

At that moment the window of the room swung open. The room was filled with an icy draught. Margaret was lifted into the air, and caterpaulted towards the window by some powerful, invisible force. Beyond the window blue-red flames lapped hungrily. The Devil had *not* gone away!

But Stephen was determined not to let it take Margaret

again. He threw himself towards the window, just in time to grab hold of Margaret's hurtling body and drag it back into the room. But the monstrous force was still pulling with ever-increasing strength, dragging her away towards the flames. His burned arms ached so much that he wanted to cry out. He must not let go! He felt himself being slowly sucked forward with her, nearer and nearer to the greedy flames.

The bewildered farm men were slow to come to Stephen's aid. Margaret was on the outer ledge of the window now. Stephen, clutching the frame with one hand to keep himself from plunging straight into the flames, could not hold her back for long. There was no way the men could reach her.

"We'll never save her!" they cried.

"We must!" shouted Stephen frantically. "Get me back into the room! I can hang on to her!"

But the invisible force was colossal. No plough stuck in a rut had ever cost the men such effort. Sweat poured down their necks and arms, and soaked their shirts. Desperately they struggled, but they could not pull Stephen back. Instead they felt him slipping slowly out of the window.

"You'll have to let her go! We can save you! She is lost!"

"No!" gasped Stephen. "You must save us both!"

"We cannot fight the Devil!"

"You must!" roared Stephen. But he knew in his heart that it was useless. The men were doing their utmost. Pain and despair were weakening his will too. He would not desert Margaret, but he could not go on fighting. He had to admit that the Devil had won.

"Let me go with her!" he called at last.

At that moment a terrible howl rent the air outside the window. Margaret, Stephen and the three farm hands tumbled backwards into the room, like a tug-of-war team when the other side suddenly lets go of the rope. A moment later Peter's face appeared in the doorway and broke into a grin of relief at the sight of them. Then the priest brushed past him and stepped into the room.

The sleeves of his cassock were singed, his wrists red and raw with burns like those that tortured Stephen. In his hands he held the deep chalice that always contained Holy Water. The bowl was almost empty. The priest dipped his finger in the tiny drop of water that remained from his battle with the Devil outside, and drew an invisible cross on Margaret's lips.

"The foul fiend is gone," he said.

The first rays of the morning sun shone through the window, warming Margaret's face. She was glad to be home from her cousin's, though she could not remember how she had got back. Stephen looked awfully tired and ill, she thought. Peter had obviously not cared for him as she would have done. The bed too was a dreadful mess. She would have to put on some fresh rosebud-embroidered pillowslips.

7

Old Nick

"I'LL THRASH you for this!"

"Eh?" Jack was still half asleep.

"I'll thrash you for this!" bellowed the squire.

Jack opened one eye and saw a crow pecking contentedly at the wheat a few feet away from him. The sun was shining on its black feathers, giving them a purple gloss. It's a lovely day, thought Jack dreamily.

A sudden blow on his shoulder spoiled this impression. Jack sat up with a start. His master was glaring down at him, brandishing a knobbly walking stick.

"You were supposed to be watching that field," he growled.

Of course, thought Jack. That was why he was sitting here. Oh dear, had he fallen asleep and failed to do his job properly *again*? Jack's eyes travelled slowly across the field of young wheat. It was covered with black dots, crows devouring the new grain.

"I'm very sorry, sir!" stuttered the boy, scrambling to

his feet half dazed with sleep. A second blow from the stick completed his awakening.

"Sorry? What's the good of being sorry when my wheat's ruined?" roared the squire, seizing hold of Jack's ear. "Look at that field! I pay you to keep your eyes on it, not to keep them shut!" The stick came down again on Jack's shoulders.

"I didn't mean to fall asleep, sir."

But his master was not interested in Jack's arguments. He hit him again and again.

"You won't go to sleep at work again in a hurry," scowled the squire, leaving off beating poor Jack at last, and stalking angrily away.

Jack wondered whether he would *ever* sleep again with his shoulders smarting so. It was too bad. He was always getting beaten on account of those crows. Last time he had got caught up in a game with some village boys. He had gone running across the meadows, forgetting all about the wheat until his master had dragged him back by the ear to see the crows dotted all over the field. This time he had been determined not to leave the field unguarded, and he hadn't. If only that wretched sun hadn't been so beautifully warm and soothing! If only sitting looking at a wheat field wasn't so boring! If only he could find a perfect way of keeping those crows off the crops!

A large black crow perched on a nearby bush, and fixed him with a beady eye.

"Would you like me to take care of the crows for you?"

Jack looked all around him for the speaker. Funny! He couldn't see anybody.

"Would you like me to take care of the crows for you?"

Jack looked again. There was definitely no one there.

"Well! Answer!"

Suddenly, to his amazement, Jack realized that the voice was coming from the crow. He had heard of parrots talking, but not crows. He stood there, gaping.

"You wouldn't like me to take care of the crows for you, then? Well! I'll be off!" The crow flapped its wings.

"No—I mean, don't go!" cried Jack in alarm. He was on the point of losing an offer of help, and help was exactly what he wanted, even if the helper was a talking crow. "Would you be able to stop them eating the crops?" he stuttered.

"Nothing simpler!"

Jack was not sure that he believed the crow. How could it have any control over the other birds?

"I have special power," said the crow, answering Jack's question even before he had asked it. Was it possible? The crow did seem to know what he was thinking. Perhaps it had other powers as well.

Jack decided to take a chance. There was a fair on at Hereford the next day, and Jack was longing to go to it. He could leave the crow in charge then.

"Tomorrow, while you're at the fair?" asked the crow, reading Jack's thoughts again.

"Yes, please!" replied Jack, already thinking happily about merry-go- rounds and skittle games.

"You'll find us all in the old barn when you get back," called the crow as it flew up and vanished into the bright blue sky.

So the next morning Jack left for Hereford with not a care in the world. It was a good ten miles from Kentchurch, the village where he lived and worked, but the weather was fine and Jack was happy. He had saved up some of his meagre wages and was intending to have a really good day.

The fair was full of marvellous things. He tried his hand at archery and won a penny whistle by hitting the target. At skittles he won a small jug of ale, which he drank secretly behind the cattle market. He had never drunk ale before and he didn't like the taste much, but when he had finished it, the fair looked even jollier than before. He watched some gaily-dressed Morris dancers with bells and tassels leaping and stamping in perfect time with each other. He rode on two different merry-go-rounds. He saw a puppet show about a fat friar, which made him laugh till his sides ached. Then he felt hungry, so he bought himself two huge jam pancakes, which were more delicious than anything he had tasted.

As he was chewing blissfully at the pancakes, he noticed a small booth which was painted black like the night and decorated with silver stars. A curtain was drawn across the front. Outside a man with brown leather skin was calling, "Learn your fortune! The gypsy woman will tell your fortune! Come inside!"

Jack stood staring at the man. He would like to know what the future had in store for him.

"Come on in, lad!"

Jack hesitated. "How much does it cost?"

"Whatever you like."

Jack had one silver threepenny bit left. He had done most of the things he wanted to do. He made up his mind. He would give it to the gypsy woman in return for knowing his fortune. He nodded to the man, who drew aside the curtain for him.

Inside was an old woman crouched behind a huge ball of crystal, which reflected her gnarled old features. A guttering candle provided a dim light.

"Sit down," said the old woman sharply. Then she was silent, gazing intently into the crystal.

Suddenly she caught her breath. She looked across at Jack in alarm.

"Beware the talking crow," she said in a voice hushed with fear.

Jack too was fearful. He had forgotten all about the wheat while he had been at the fair. Perhaps the crow had let him down. Perhaps he would return to the farm and find the wheat field covered in crows, and his master angrier than ever.

"Has it played a trick on me?" he blurted out.

"Not yet!" replied the old gypsy. "But listen to what I have to say. Do not give the crow what it wants tonight. Even so, you will not be easily rid of it. It will come after you again and again. Be always alert. Do not let it see what you are thinking."

The woman's voice was urgent, her old face anxious. She peered nervously into the crystal. At last her face relaxed.

"Throw the dog's bone on to the bridge," she said. She held out her hand to receive Jack's threepence.

It was rather a waste of money, thought Jack as he left the booth. At first the gypsy had had something interesting to say, but that stuff about the dog and its bone was daft. What about his future? She hadn't said anything useful. He would have done much better to have had some more turns on the merry-go-round.

Just then he felt a heavy hand on his shoulder. He turned round and saw his master's face, scarlet with fury.

"Who's looking after my wheat?" he growled.

"A crow," replied Jack, hoping that the crow had kept its promise, and not thinking that his answer sounded silly.

JANE EDMONDS

The squire looked as if he was about to explode.

"Don't you try to make fun of me!" He raised his stick.

"I—I'm not, sir. The crow said it would take care of things for me."

Wham! The stick came down mercilessly on Jack's back.

"It talked to you, did it?" His master raised the stick again.

"Yes!" cried Jack.

The squire lowered the stick without hitting him and stared at the boy. In spite of the absurd story, he did not look as though he was lying. Jack seized the moment to explain further.

"The crows are all in the old barn. If you like I can show you," he added timidly. If only the crow had not failed him!

"Very well," said his master, surprised at his own weakness, and resolving to thrash Jack even harder if his story turned out to be untrue, which it almost certainly would. He marched Jack to his cart, and they drove back to Kentchurch in silence.

Jack was beginning to feel very unhappy. The gypsy had said, "*Beware the talking crow.*" Now the crow had a chance to harm him. The gypsy said that the crow had not yet tricked him, but it could well have done so by the time they got to the barn.

He held his breath as they trundled up the farm lane. He could just see the wheat field in the distance. Then his face broke into a grin. There was not a single black dot to be seen.

But as they approached the barn, he began to feel anxious again. He could not hear anything. Surely those noisy, squawking crows would not be sitting there in silence. He looked across at his master, whose face was set and grim. If the barn were empty, he could expect no mercy. The squire pulled the horse to a halt.

"Come with me," he snapped. He jumped down from the cart and marched into the barn. Warily Jack followed him.

"Where are they then?" demanded the squire.

A sudden squawk came from above their heads. They both looked up. The rafters of the barn were covered with crows, sitting in docile silence. A great wave of relief swept through Jack. The talking crow had not let him down. He grinned triumphantly at his master. The squire looked back at him with respect almost fear. He decided it would be wiser never to raise his stick to Jack again.

"One good turn deserves another," said the crow, perching beside Jack as soon as the squire was safely out of the way.

"Certainly!" replied Jack, quite forgetting the gypsy's warning. "What do you want?"

"Your soul!"

What a strange thing! What use was his soul to a talking crow. Then it began to dawn on Jack who this curious creature was. The old woman's words were ringing in his ears now. "*Do not give the crow what it wants tonight.*" He certainly wouldn't. There was only one person who could possibly want his soul, and that was Old Nick, the Devil. Jack shook his head violently. To his relief the crow fluttered off without another word.

Jack soon forgot all about this first encounter with the Devil. The Devil did not forget. He was angry that he had spent a whole day sitting in the barn with a gaggle of crows for nothing, and he was determined to get his revenge. But he waited several years, until Jack was grown up and owner of a small farm on the outskirts of Kentchurch.

JACK WAS going to market to buy some pigs. On his way he became aware of a stranger walking a little way behind him. The man was exceptionally swarthy, with black beady eyes and black hair. He was dressed like a farmer; probably bound for the market as well, thought Jack. He looked rich. It would be nice to make some money, reflected Jack enviously.

"I was about to suggest a little business deal," said the stranger without introducing himself. "I'm sure it would be greatly to your advantage."

"Really?" replied Jack eagerly. It was as though the beady-eyed farmer had known what was on his mind. "What kind of a deal?"

What happened next was still more amazing. The farmer took a bag of gold from his pocket and tossed it to Jack.

"Pigs," said the farmer. "Put this with your own money and buy a fine herd. Then we'll divide it between us."

Jack gasped. The bag of gold would buy ten times as many pigs as his own small savings. The deal certainly would be to his advantage. He wondered how the farmer had guessed he was going to buy pigs. He really seemed to see straight into Jack's mind.

Jack had a strange feeling that this mind-reading had happened before, but he could not recall when. Then with a start he remembered. "*It will come after you again and again. Do not let it see what you are thinking.*" Of course, the crow, Old . . . But Jack did not add the name "Nick", even in his mind. He covered his thoughts with a hurried speech. "But how shall we divide the pigs? You are paying so much more than me!"

"Personally, I like a bit of a gamble," replied the farmer. Thank goodness! He had not seen that Jack had recognized him. "Suppose I take all the pigs with straight tails? You can have the ones with curly tails."

"Sounds reasonable," said Jack. But he had never seen a pig with a straight tail, unless it was cold, miserable or sick. Why should Old Nick be so generous? Probably he intended to put a spell on the pigs to straighten their tails. Hurriedly Jack went on talking, "... very reasonable but rather to your disadvantage. As I'm putting less money towards them, I think I should take the pigs with the straight tails." Hidden behind these words, a plan was taking shape.

The Devil was astonished. Pigs' tails could not be straight without a spell. Still, if Jack were that foolish, he could do him out of his pigs without even the bother of making one.

"Very well," he agreed. "I'll meet you here when you've come back from the market."

About a hundred yards ahead was the river Monnow, with a small wooden footbridge slung across it. Jack pointed to the bridge.

"I'd sooner meet there," he said. "Just this side of the bridge. It's a good place to herd the pigs if you're late," he added by way of explanation.

Jack bought a magnificent herd of pigs at the market. Without exception they had healthy curly tails, but Jack was not bothered by this. He set off back to Kentchurch, hardly able to keep himself from chuckling. He took the longest way back, through winding muddy lanes. The poor animals wore themselves out, slithering and sliding over pebbly hills and down waterlogged valleys. But Jack ignored their tiredness. He drove them along at merciless speed, without stopping to feed them. They began to look dejected. Jack refused to allow himself to feel sorry for them. Any pity would ruin his plan.

At last the wooden bridge came into view. Jack was relieved to see that the farmer had not yet arrived at their meeting place on the other side. He guided the pigs towards the bridge, but, just before they reached it, turned them sharply and drove them, squealing and complaining, through the icy water. They gathered on the far bank, a cold, miserable bunch. Their tails drooped down like dead worms. At that moment the farmer appeared.

"I'm afraid they all seem to have straight tails," said Jack innocently.

"You've cheated me!" roared the farmer.

"How could you say such a thing!" exclaimed Jack indignantly, wondering whether Old Nick knew he was recognized. "It just happens that all the pigs at the market seem to have straight tails today."

It was very tempting, after this first success, to try and trick the Devil again, so Jack did not stop. "If you like to let me have some more money, I'll go back to the market and buy another lot of pigs. As you haven't done well out of the first deal, I'll let you have the straight-tailed pigs next time."

The Devil did not know that Jack had seen through his disguise. This was his chance to make up for his losses. He tossed Jack a second bag of gold coins.

Jack drove his first herd of pigs home, then set off to buy another. He was confident that he would be rich before the day was out.

This time he took an easy route back to the bridge. He

allowed the pigs to trot along at a leisurely pace, munching any tasty roots they found on the way. Shortly before they reached the bridge, he gave them an enormous feed of beans. Then he drove them over the bridge, taking care that none of them went near the icy water. Their tails were curled tight with the joy and comfort of being well-cared-for pigs. Not a single tail could possibly be called straight.

When the farmer saw them, he gave a diabolical howl of dismay, forgot all about his disguise, and vanished, leaving Jack one of the wealthiest farmers in Herefordshire.

Jack was so rich that he was not surprised to be visited one day by a farm bailiff, who told him that he would have to pay some taxes. The bailiff, who had a sharp, beak-like nose, explained that he had been sent by his master, the Bishop of Hereford. He did not want money, however. He wanted the crop from Jack's largest field.

"That's all my wheat." Jack stared at him in dismay.

"I regret so," replied the beak-nosed bailiff sympathetically.

Jack shrugged his shoulders. There was no point in saying no. He was bound to have to pay up in the long run. It was curious that the bailiff should come for the crop so early in the year, though. Surely he did not want to take the tender green shoots that were just beginning to peep through the soil.

"Oh no! I'll come back for the wheat when it's ripe," the bailiff replied to this thought.

Jack knew in a flash who the bailiff was. "*It will come after you again and again.*" The old gypsy woman's prophecy was proving startlingly exact. "*Be always alert,*" she had said.

"Very well," Jack replied to the bailiff quickly in order

not to arouse his suspicions. "I'll have it ready for you." Then he added with a friendly smile, "Would you like to see the field?"

"Perhaps I should," agreed the bailiff, trying to sound official.

Jack took him to see his second largest field. "You think this will suit you?" he asked.

"Excellent!" said the bailiff, delighted to have fooled Jack with such ease this time.

"You won't object if I ask you to leave me the roots?" said Jack reasonably.

"Have them by all means," replied the bailiff, feeling generous, and he left the farm rubbing his hands with glee.

The harvest came and Jack filled twenty sacks with full-grown shoots for the bailiff, who came for them with a horse and cart. One by one the bailiff loaded the sacks on to the cart. They were heavy and it took a long time, but Jack did not help. He stood and watched and concentrated on other things, just in case the bailiff should try any thought-reading and uncover Jack's secret before he had loaded the last sack.

As soon as the bailiff was out of sight, Jack's face broke into an enormous grin. He went round to the back of his barn to admire his crop of turnips. These were the roots from the field he had shown the bailiff. When Old Nick opened his sacks, he would find nothing but turnip tops.

The bailiff came back the very same day. He was very angry. He would have Jack brought before the assizes for trying to avoid the tax.

Jack apologetically replied that the bailiff himself had let him keep the roots of the crop; but if the bailiff had got into trouble with the Bishop, he would try and make amends by letting him have the crop of a neighbouring field which he would be harvesting in a couple of months.

The Devil was suspicious. "Show me the field," he said dourly.

Jack did as he was told. The field looked the same as the other one, with green shoots peeping through the soil.

"I expect you want to take the roots this time," said Jack understandingly.

"I certainly do!" snapped the bailiff, ignoring Jack's friendly smile. He would get the better of this man yet!

This time Jack did not even bother to put the bailiff's share in sacks. He just left the stubble in the field after he had reaped the grain-filled ears of wheat for himself.

"There are your roots," he told the bailiff when he came back for his second crop, pointing to the bare field.

The Devil gave a howl of anger and frustration, and the beak-nosed bailiff vanished, as the beady-eyed farmer had done.

The Devil was not sure that he had been recognized, but he suspected it. He therefore waited several years before he visited Jack again. He had another reason, too. He hated Jack for the tricks he had played, and he did not intend to pay him out with a mere joke. His revenge would be cruel and deadly, and it would be easier when Jack was no longer young.

IT WAS not long until Jack's sixtieth birthday, but he was still healthy and active. Indeed, he had recently built a grand new barn without any help at all. One morning, as he was walking through the yard on his way to feed the pigs, he found a swarthy man with black hair admiring the barn. The man looked like a builder.

"That's a fine piece of workmanship," said the man, nodding at the new building. "Who built it?"

"I did," said Jack. He couldn't help feeling rather pleased.

"Remarkable!" said the man. "I'm a builder by trade, and I've never seen work like that before."

Jack glowed with pride as the builder went on, "I suppose you wouldn't like to give me a hand with a job I've got to get done in a hurry? It's rather a lot for me on my own. I'll pay you very well, as you are so skilled." He held out a purse full of coins.

Although he was rich, Jack was never one to turn down money. Besides, he was flattered by the man's words.

"It would be a pleasure," he agreed. The man tossed him the purse. It was full of gold.

The job turned out to be a stone bridge over the River Monnow. Jack and the builder worked hard without breaking for food or drink, and by the end of the first day it was half finished. Worn out, Jack laid down his tools.

"Surely you're not stopping already?" said the builder.

"I am!" Jack replied firmly. He had not really enjoyed the day. When he had built his barn, he had allowed himself frequent rests. The builder was a slave-driver.

"But we'd only take the night to get it all finished," coaxed the builder.

"And I'd be finished too," replied Jack. "I'm not young any more."

The builder grinned slyly to himself.

"I'll give you another purse of gold if you work tonight," he said, and held out a purse that looked even heavier than the first.

Jack was tempted. But his back ached with tiredness. A night's work after the strenuous day would exhaust him. It was not worth ruining his health, even for that fat purse. He refused. The builder looked angry for a moment, then his face brightened. Jack would still not come out of this encounter alive.

"I'll see you here tomorrow then," he said, trying to look friendly.

Jack still felt very tired as he walked towards the bridge the next morning. The thought of another day's unbroken labour weighed heavily upon him. However, he comforted himself with the thought that they should finish the bridge by nightfall. He looked across to the bridge, glad that he had done so much the day before.

What he saw made him gasp with horror. The bridge was in ruins. Stones lay smashed on the river bank. The pillars were nothing more than crumbling mounds, over which the water washed undisturbed. The builder was sitting on the bank, gazing dismally at the devastation.

"We'll just have to start all over again," he said.

Jack's heart sank. "How did it happen?" he said dolefully.

"It must have been the storm in the night," replied the builder.

Storm? Had there been a storm? Jack had not heard it. He must have been so tired that he had slept right through it. He had never done that before. His farmer's ears usually listened anxiously for the slightest growl of thunder.

"We'd better build it more soundly this time," he said with a weary sigh.

"My opinion exactly!" said the builder, looking surprisingly cheerful and springing up with great energy.

But Jack had the feeling that he was working harder than the builder that day. The builder did a lot of scurrying to and fro, but it was Jack who really laboured with care and effort.

Nevertheless, by the end of the day the bridge had reached the same point as it had the evening before. The only difference was that Jack was feeling even more tired. He ached from head to foot. He could not stand up without his head spinning. He walked unsteadily.

"I really think we should work through the night," said the builder. "If we finish the bridge there will be no danger of its being broken up by another storm."

It was very unlikely that there would be so strong a storm again, thought Jack. Besides, he felt so weak. He doubted whether he would have the strength to stagger home, let alone to continue working throughout the night.

"I'm afraid I must rest," said Jack, sitting down on the bank. His joints creaked painfully.

"Already?" said the builder, looking disappointed.

But there was no reply. Jack had slumped forward; his whole body rolled over sideways. The builder looked at him eagerly; then his face fell. Jack was breathing steadily. He was only asleep.

When Jack awoke, the first thing he saw was the bridge: shattered! With a cry of dismay, he struggled to his feet.

"What happened this time?"

"Another storm," replied the builder solemnly. Jack stared at him in disbelief. How could he not have woken up? Why were his clothes still dry?

"It happened early on," explained the builder. "Your coat has dried out since."

But Jack had not asked his question out loud. The builder had replied to his thought alone. The crow . . . the farmer . . . the bailiff . . . now Jack knew who the builder was! Old

Nick had been clever this time. Or was he, Jack, getting old and unobservant? And what was the Devil trying to do with this bridge that he demolished each night?

"We'd better set to work again," said the builder enthusiastically.

Just in order that you can smash it up again? thought Jack. I'm not that stupid.

"I'm afraid I'm too tired," he told the builder.

The builder frowned; but the angry look passed quickly as he drew out the largest purse of gold that Jack had yet seen.

He doesn't give up easily, Jack thought. If I were younger I'd take him on again. He remembered his previous victories over Old Nick. It would be nice to score over him just once more. The idea of such a challenge revived him.

"I've changed my mind," he declared, taking the gold.

This time Jack had not troubled to disguise his thoughts. The Devil knew he was recognized, and he knew how Jack planned to foil him. The plan was simple: Jack would finish the bridge, take home the gold and have a good laugh at Old Nick's expense. But it was the Devil who was laughing. He was dealing with a tired old man, too exhausted to think clearly.

Jack worked with a will, in spite of his aching limbs. The Devil just watched. He was longing for the bridge to be finished, for the bridge itself was the trap in which he would catch Jack. The soul of the first person to step on to it would belong to him; and with Jack growing feebler every minute, he was sure Jack would be that person. It was a satisfying revenge, to see Jack labouring so hard to build his own death and damnation.

Jack did not stop working at nightfall, even though his

earlier burst of energy was long past and he felt more ill than on either of the previous two nights. Only his will-power kept him going, heaving stone on to stone, tearing his poor muscles and straining his chest so that it hurt him constantly.

He finished the bridge just before daybreak. With a sigh of relief, he stepped back to admire his handiwork. But suddenly, his vision was blurred. A terrible pain jabbed at his heart. His hands and feet were overtaken by a creeping numbness. Had he worked himself to death? Was that what the Devil had wanted? Had Old Nick won the last round after all?

"Step on to my bridge!" The builder's voice came through to him murkily. Muddled and sick as he was, Jack immediately suspected the command. Why should Old Nick want him to do that? Was the old crow still after his soul?

"I can't. I'm too weak," he muttered feebly. "You try it. It's your bridge."

As Jack said these words, the pain lessened. He could see again. The builder was standing close beside him, frowning.

"I'll try it after you," he said, taking Jack's arm and propelling him towards the bridge. "Let me help you."

Jack wrenched himself away, setting off another agonizing pain in his chest. He sank to the ground, trying to catch his breath. The builder loomed threateningly above him.

Then the builder turned round. A small brown and white dog was snapping at his heels, trying to reach an old bone that the builder was treading into the ground.

Jack watched the builder try to kick the dog away, but the little animal kept coming back. I wonder why he doesn't just throw him the bone, thought Jack, his enfeebled mind wandering carelessly.

Then a hammering began in his head, "*Throw the bone . . . throw the bone . . . throw—*" Why were the words so familiar and so urgent? If only he could think properly! Painfully, Jack reached out his hand and curled his fingers round the bone, hoping that it might help him to remember. At the same moment the Devil turned back to him, and taking him by the shoulders, heaved him to his feet. Jack, still clutching the bone, felt himself dragged forward . . .

"*. . . on to the bridge*"—the gypsy's words! The message had come at last! He knew now what he had to do if he could. He was less than a step away from the bridge now. Bound as much by his own lack of strength as by the Devil's hands, he cast the bone feebly forward. It just reached the edge of the bridge, then slithered a few inches across the stone. There was a sound of yapping, and the little dog shot past him, pouncing eagerly on the bone.

No sooner had the dog's feet touched the bridge than it vanished. Jack collapsed on the river bank and fell into a painless sleep.

The Devil left him sleeping there. There was no point in struggling further: his bridge could claim only one soul, and it had got that—the soul of a dog. He did not even howl diabolically, but sighed with misery, anger and disappointment. Then he vanished, like the dog.

8

The Temptress

THE CHALICE glowed red-hot. Dunstan was glowing too with the heat of the furnace and with pleasure in his craft. The golden chalice would be the most beautiful thing he had ever made.

It was a relief to get away from the other monks for a while. Sometimes Dunstan felt very tired of seeing the same faces and hearing the same dreary talk. He remembered with longing the days when, as a boy, he had gone running across the fields to swim in clear, blue pools, when laughter filled the air and soft breezes caressed his face. He dreamed sadly of the girls he had met when he was living at King Athelstan's court, where life had seemed so gay. But then he reminded himself sternly that he had made a solemn vow to give up all the pleasures of the world, and to dedicate his life to loving and serving God alone.

No one knew about these wistful daydreams, and Dunstan wished he could conquer them. When they came he would escape quietly to his tiny forge beside the Abbey, where he could lose himself completely in his work and forget his dissatisfaction.

He was feeling better already. He would just have time to finish the chalice before Vespers. He set to work with his mallet, shaping the cup lovingly.

Suddenly he felt that someone was watching him. Impossible! The monks all knew that the forge was his private territory. Besides, he had not heard the door open or close; no draught had disturbed the fire. Dunstan did not even bother to look up from his work.

But the feeling that he was not alone grew stronger and stronger. It was hard to concentrate. His mallet slipped, making an ugly dent in the chalice. He looked up.

What he saw made him drop his mallet altogether, denting the gold worse than before. Standing no more than a foot away from him was a girl of about eighteen, slim and pale, with raven-black hair that fell thickly upon her shoulders like a curtain of shimmering satin. Dunstan had not really expected to see anything at all. He was stunned at the sight of the girl, and angry. How dare she walk into the Abbey! How dare she intrude upon his work!

"How did you come in here? Go away!" he snapped. The girl winced and took a step back towards the door.

"I'm very sorry," she said. She hesitated, her hand on the door handle, then turned towards Dunstan, wanting to explain. "I was passing. I saw the light of your fire." She spoke in short, nervous bursts. "I wondered what it could be. So I came in. You can't have heard me when I knocked at the door." She stared at Dunstan anxiously. "You were so busy with your work. I've been watching you for ages," she added. "You're wonderfully clever."

As he listened to her soft voice, so timid and flattering,

Dunstan felt his anger lessening. His first shock was giving way to wonder at her beauty. Her eyes, gazing at him fearfully, were blue and shining, reminding him of clear pools on a summer's day.

"I'll go now." She opened the door of the forge. Through it Dunstan glimpsed a brilliant sky, the exact colour of her eyes.

"Well—perhaps you may stay," admitted Dunstan, adding very casually, "you won't be in my way."

The girl quickly closed the door again. "You're quite sure?" she asked in her shy voice.

"Yes," Dunstan nodded, trying not to sound too willing. He gave her the wooden stool that he usually sat on himself. Then he turned purposefully back to his work.

The chalice had cooled down while he was talking to the girl. It was impossible to shape it any more without reheating it. He took his tongs and lifted it into the furnace.

The girl stared at him admiringly with her blue-pool eyes. He did his utmost not to look at her, and to think only about what he was doing. He turned his back on her, but still he felt those eyes upon him. He longed to return her gaze, but he knew that such longing was dangerous. The girl came from the world he had vowed to give up, the world of freedom and delight and summer laughter.

Although his eyes had been fixed firmly upon the furnace, Dunstan had not been able to stop thinking about the girl, and he had failed to notice what was happening to the chalice. With a jolt he realized that the metal had overheated and was even beginning to melt on one side. He jerked it hurriedly out of the fire and plunged it into the tub of water that stood next to the furnace. It sank down hissing, as if in anger at the careless treatment it had received. Dunstan's work was ruined.

There was no point in going on. Dunstan thrust the tongs back into the fire. Then he turned round to face the girl.

"I'm afraid my work isn't very good today." He took the chalice out of the water and put it on his work shelf. It was the worst thing he had ever made—a lumpy, misshapen pot.

"I think it's wonderful." The blue eyes sparkled with admiration. Dunstan felt better. Perhaps the chalice wasn't such a disaster after all, and he was judging it too severely. He looked at it again. It was *almost* round. "Wonderful" was the word the girl had used. Dunstan began to feel pleased with himself. The chalice was not at all bad—quite good, really.

"Do you make many beautiful things like that?" asked the girl.

He smiled at her proudly. She was right, he thought, the chalice was beautiful in a way.

"As many as I can."

She was sitting on the stool he had given her. He could just see her slender ankles beneath the hem of her white dress. She was lovelier than any of the girls at the King's court.

"Being a goldsmith is a pleasant change for a monk!" he said.

"Do monks need a change?" asked the girl innocently.

"Sometimes I do." Dunstan had never admitted that to anyone before.

"Why?" The girl was so straightforward and without guile. To Dunstan she seemed perfect in every way.

"Because I never meet anyone like you." What was he saying? A monk who had vowed to serve God faithfully!

The girl laughed prettily. "Well, you've met me now. Does that make you happier?"

"Yes!" Dunstan replied gaily. What did it matter? He wasn't being serious. He was only flirting with the girl. But a monk flirting? Was that right? It couldn't do much harm, Dunstan decided. He was happy talking to this charming girl, admiring her beauty. Surely God could not grudge him that after so many years' devoted service.

Dunstan talked to the girl as he had never talked to anyone in his life before—of his childhood, of his life at court, of the monastery, even of the boredom and discontent that sometimes oppressed him. The girl listened with such interest and concern that it seemed to Dunstan that he was talking to an old friend. He felt a warmth that he had never known before. The blue eyes that watched him so intently, the pale face, fragile in its frame of black hair, stirred in him a new feeling that was forbidden by his vows—love for a woman.

Bells were ringing, summoning the monks to Vespers. Why did they jangle so harshly in his ears, when usually they sounded so beautiful? Was it because they were calling him away from the girl? Reluctantly Dunstan stepped towards the door.

The blue eyes filled with tears. "Are you leaving me?"

"I must!"

"Why?"

"I have to go to Vespers."

"Why?" The girl sounded petulant, like a spoiled child. Dunstan tried to explain: all the monks would expect him; God would expect him. If he were not in the Abbey his reputation, perhaps even his soul, would suffer. The girl was less understanding now, and only interested in getting her own way. She stood up, pouting tearfully.

"If you go, you will never see me again."

The threat was like a knife poised at his heart.

"And that would make me very unhappy," she added in a voice that was suddenly gentle and appealing again. Dunstan could have resisted her anger, but he could not resist her sadness. He hated himself for upsetting her. How could he be so cruel? Surely God would not wish that!

"I'll stay a little longer," he said. The girl's face brightened. It was as if the sun had come out after a storm, promising pleasure and gaiety. She stepped towards him with bright, laughing eyes, and wound her arms around his neck.

They stood there without moving. Dunstan was enchanted.

But this happiness lasted only until the bells stopped ringing. Vespers would begin at any moment. The monks would be wondering why he was not there.

"I must go now! I'm already late!" he exclaimed.

"No!" The girl's arms tightened against his neck almost unpleasantly. Dunstan tried to loosen her grip, but in vain.

"I shan't let you go now." Her voice was firm, like her clasp. Then, once again, it became soft and pleasing. "I know you really want to stay with me."

Dunstan gazed down at the blue eyes, so adoring and anxious. She was telling the truth—he did want to stay. Perhaps God *would* understand, he thought.

"Yes," he said weakly, "I do."

Her grip on his neck relaxed.

The girl turned towards the door and opened it wide. Light summer air filled the forge, cooling Dunstan's face. Emerald grass gleamed in the bright sunshine. A lark was singing. The girl smiled at Dunstan, radiant like the day she had let in. He was spellbound.

"I should like you to stay with me for ever," she whispered. "Come away with me now."

The monks were all at Vespers. He had only to walk through that open door and run away across the fields. What was there to stop him, except his vow to love and serve God? Could he break that? Did God know about falling in love?

"I will make you so happy," pleaded the girl.

Dunstan turned away, trying to think clearly. He looked round the tiny forge with its furnace and its single wooden stool. He was happy here, but there had been bleak lonely times as well. He thought of the monotony of his days, the simple food, the sombre darkness and the long silences. Was that what God wanted of him for the rest of his life?

A few steps and he would be free! He would be able to begin a new life with this beautiful girl. He turned back to the girl.

"I will come away with you," he said.

"For ever and ever?" she asked, her eyes bright with hope.

"Yes. For ever and ever."

"You promise?"

"I promise."

The blue eyes glittered with delight. Dunstan bent down joyfully to kiss the pale brow, then suddenly drew back, catching his breath. The eyes had changed. It seemed to Dunstan that the warm, sunny, blue pools had frozen over. He saw in them not love, but triumph.

"Come on!" The girl clasped his hand.

But something held him back. She was as beautiful as she had been two minutes ago, yet now her hands seemed clawing, her smile greedy. She reminded Dunstan of a serpent about to wind itself around its prey.

The girl tugged at his hand. He did not move.

"Have you changed your mind?" she hissed.

The girl he had loved a moment ago now filled him with dread; as if behind the pale mask of her face there lurked an appalling danger.

"I must," he said.

"But you gave me your promise!"

"I gave God my promise too!" cried Dunstan desperately, shrinking away from her.

"Never mind about God," mocked the girl, gripping his hand more tightly. "You belong to me now!"

Panic seized him like a vicious cramp. He tried to shake his hand free. The girl's grasp only tightened. She began to laugh—a loud, rasping, evil laugh. His hand was agony; razor claws were driving into it. His strength began to ebb away.

He knew now that this beautiful girl who had seemed so innocent, to whom he had promised himself for ever, was none other than the Devil.

Overwhelmed with despair, Dunstan raised his free hand. The girl's eyes flashed jubilantly. In that second he hated her far more than he had loved her. How could he fight the Devil, powerless as he was?

Perhaps it was God who guided his eyes towards the furnace and the tongs that were lying in it. With sudden hope, Dunstan reached out and snatched them from the fire, and, before the girl realized what was happening, thrust the red-hot pincers into her beautiful face, clamping them on to her delicate nose.

The girl screamed, an agonized screech of pain that

JANE EDMONDS

blasted across the countryside and terrified all that heard it. Her features began to melt into a new shape—huge, menacing, loathsome, a great, scaly serpent with murky blood-red eyes—the Devil himself!

Dunstan dropped the tongs and turned away, unable to face the fiend that would destroy him.

The scream stopped. Dunstan was doomed to death and Hell. He waited for the torment to begin.

Nothing happened.

At length Dunstan dared to turn his head. He was quite alone. The tongs were lying on the floor. On his work shelf stood a very shoddy golden chalice.

He took up the tongs and lifted the golden cup into the furnace. He would have to begin shaping it all over again.

This time he was not disturbed. The Devil was many miles away, trying to cool his nose.

9

A Dangerous Bargain

THE MAYOR of Aix walked gloomily into the cathedral—a magnificent monument to the glory of God and Emperor Charles the Great, and the pride and joy of the City of Aix. At least, that was what it was meant to be. A drop of rain landed on the Mayor's nose, and gave a cool reminder that it was unlikely to be either of those things.

The cathedral had no roof. Not even the walls were complete. And there was no money to add a single stone to the unfinished building, let alone to pay for gold and glass and all the other costly things that an emperor's cathedral would be expected to have. The Mayor scraped a lump of moss from one of the great pillars. It wasn't his fault; but it was his worry. The Emperor had left him, as chief of the town council, in charge of the building, while he had gone off to fight the Saxons. He expected to find the cathedral finished when he got back. But the Emperor also needed a great deal of money to wage his Saxon war. The royal treasury was empty. The people's pockets were empty, for they had already paid everything they had in war taxes.

The whole city was broke. There was nothing left for the cathedral. And the Mayor had an uncomfortable feeling that he would get the blame. He crushed the moss in the palm of his hand, just as an emperor might crush an unsatisfactory mayor. Then he hurried out of the cathedral and along the street leading to the council chamber.

The councillors were meeting to discuss the problem of the cathedral. It was the only thing they did discuss these days, and they discussed it every day. They had not yet thought of anything. But it was comforting to pretend that they were doing something about it.

There was a hush as the Mayor entered the room. He guessed that his fellow councillors had been saying something unpleasant about him, probably blaming him for having found no way out of their difficulty. He sat down and listened as they resumed their discussion.

"We could persuade the builders to work for nothing!"

"They have no materials."

"The builders have all left the city."

"Can we not explain to the Emperor? Perhaps he will sympathize with us."

"Perhaps he will have us executed!" The Mayor's voice rang out, forcing the councillors to realize the danger they were in. The councillors stared at him angrily. He had only said what they were all afraid of; but they preferred to hide such horrible thoughts at the back of their minds.

"We must borrow some money," the Mayor went on desperately. "If we don't get that cathedral finished, we're all done for. We have to get money, even if it comes from the Devil himself."

The laughter stopped abruptly. Whatever they might

think of him, the Mayor was right. The councillors all knew it.

Soberly, they began racking their brains as to how they could find a moneylender rich enough to pay for a cathedral.

After five hopeless hours of puzzling and arguing, they were about to adjourn the council till the following day, when they heard a gentle tap on the door.

"Come in," said the Mayor nervously. He was constantly expecting an ambassador from the Emperor, sent to check on the cathedral's progress.

The door opened and a stranger entered. The Mayor felt his heart hammering frantically against his ribs. This man might well come from the Emperor; he was certainly of high enough rank to be an important messenger. He was dressed magnificently, in a long gown of purple velvet, stitched with silver and ornamented with pearls the size of grapes. The gown was belted tightly into his slim waist by a broad band of gold, from which flashed emeralds, rubies and sapphires. Around his neck hung a heavy gold chain, a hundred times finer than the one the Mayor wore with such pride. He was without doubt a very grand lord. The Mayor stood up and bowed meekly, signalling to his councillors to do likewise.

"Please don't stand for my sake," said the stranger pleasantly. The Mayor felt reassured. Surely no Imperial ambassador would be so unceremonious. He nodded to the councillors to be seated, and offered a chair to the magnificent visitor, who accepted it graciously.

"You must wonder who I am and why I'm here," said the stranger.

The Mayor nodded.

"It concerns your cathedral."

The Mayor's heart began hammering again. The Emperor *must* have sent him.

"Don't worry! I don't come from the Emperor Charles." The stranger seemed to know what the Mayor was thinking.

"I came because I heard you were in trouble," said the visitor with a sympathetic smile. "I thought I might be able to help you."

"You mean—lend us some money?" stammered the Mayor, hardly daring to believe his ears.

"I'll give you some if you like," said the stranger casually.

It was as if a great weight had been lifted from the Mayor's shoulders. The councillors around him thanked the stranger from the bottom of their hearts. The magnificent gentleman sat silent, smiling at them benignly. Nevertheless, the Mayor had to be practical.

"How much will you give us?" he inquired cautiously.

"Whatever you need," replied the generous stranger. It was almost too good to be true.

"And you don't want anything in return?" asked the Mayor incredulously.

"Nothing substantial!" The stranger spoke almost too casually. The Mayor felt suddenly uneasy.

"What does that mean?" he demanded.

"It means that I want nothing that will cost you time, effort or money."

"Then what will it cost us?" the Mayor wanted to know, still more troubled.

"A soul!"

The Mayor caught his breath. The councillors' faces around him were puzzled and alarmed. An icy shiver crept down his spine, his limbs felt weak. Surely this magnificent gentleman . . .? The Mayor remembered now what he had said in council only a few hours ago: "We have to get money, even if it comes from . . ."

"I suppose you thought I had horns and a great forked tail," said the stranger, cutting into his thoughts.

There was no doubt now who this splendid, generous gentleman was. The councillors' faces were grey with horror. They clutched their sides, fearful lest at any moment Satan should reach out and wrench the soul from within him, each one hoping that the Devil's eye would light on someone else.

Satan looked on amused. People often recoiled from him like this, but they usually recovered after a while. He only had to wait.

At last the Mayor managed to speak—a feeble croak from a throat parched by fear.

"Whose soul?"

"The first soul to enter the cathedral once it is finished."

A huge sigh of relief engulfed the chamber; the men were released from their terror. The Devil was not demanding one of *their* souls after all. A sudden buzz of discussion filled the council chamber. Mayor and councillors were all agreed that Satan's offer was the only answer to their problem, but they were nonetheless worried about accepting it. They knew in their hearts that it was dangerous to deal with the Devil. They also knew that, even if none of their souls was to be sacrificed immediately, the day would come when Satan's demand would have to be met.

"I'm offering a marvellous bargain," interrupted the Devil. "Think of the souls that the cathedral will save once it is finished! Millions of them! And I am only asking for one."

He's right there, thought the Mayor. The councillors nodded their agreement.

"And I am being extremely generous," continued Satan, pleased to see that his argument was working well. "In exchange for that one soul, I am willing to give you unlimited money. Of course," he added slyly, "I shall be much better off if you refuse, as I shall be able to use the money to buy souls in the streets of your city. I should get at least a hundred for a sum like that."

Just one soul instead of a hundred, thought the Mayor. It seemed very reasonable. The councillors were nodding enthusiastically now.

"I'll help you with the building, too," went on the Devil eagerly. "I'll make the door for the West side of the cathedral myself. Besides, not one of you is anxious to be executed by the Emperor. I am offering to save your lives."

That was the most persuasive point of all. The Mayor looked round at the faces of the councillors; he could see that they were all in agreement; it was both right and sensible to accept the offer.

"We agree," he said to Satan with a grateful smile.

"Very wise," replied the Devil, placing an official-looking parchment in front of the Mayor. "Please be so kind as to sign this."

The Mayor read the document quickly. It contained nothing more than the terms of their agreement. Yet he could not suppress a shudder.

"I, Satan, do solemnly promise to provide sufficient money for the completion of the Cathedral of Aix-la-Chapelle. In return, we, the Mayor and Councillors of that same town, do promise Satan the first soul that enters the Cathedral after its completion."

The Mayor's hand shook as he signed his name, almost as if it were trying to prevent him from writing. When he passed the parchment to the councillors he noticed that they too had difficulty in signing.

As soon as they had finished Satan snatched back the document. In exchange he gave the Mayor another—an exact copy. The only difference was the signature. It was a crucifix, upside down.

The deal was done. Satan bowed politely and left the council chamber.

Then the councillors heard a curious chinking sound coming from the walls of the chamber. Gold coins were plopping on to the floor like raindrops. They came faster and faster, pouring out now from walls and ceiling, hitting the councillors on their heads, noses, eyes, chins, hands, feet, knees, ears, toes, fingers, thumbs; a great hailstorm of guilders and ducats. Soon the councillors were wading knee-deep in gold. Not one of them doubted now; they had made the right decision.

Nevertheless, the Mayor proposed, and all the council agreed, that it was wise to keep their agreement a secret.

Work on the cathedral began the next day. The Council of Aix was able to employ hundreds of skilled craftsmen and to buy all the costly materials they needed. The townspeople were delighted. Not only had they been spared the Emperor's wrath, but there was plenty of well-paid work for everybody. Whenever the Mayor or one of his councillors was seen in the town, a cheer would go up for the "saviours of Aix".

But then a strange rumour began in the city, and within a fortnight all the citizens of Aix knew indisputably that the price they had to pay for their cathedral was a soul, and that

JANE EDMONDS.

the merchant with whom their trusted Mayor and councillors had trafficked was the Devil. The cheers turned to boos. At first people demanded their resignation, imprisonment and execution. Then they began to insist that the promised soul must belong either to the Mayor or to one of the councillors who had signed the agreement with Satan.

In panic the council returned to its daily discussions. The pattern never varied. They all agreed that a soul must be found. They even admitted that it was right that one of them should provide the soul. But which one? For nobody would admit that the soul should be his own.

The question grew daily more urgent. The cathedral was almost finished. No moss grew within its walls now. But the Mayor, standing in the kaleidoscope light of its glass windows, was as unhappy as he had been when no roof had kept out the raindrops. In a few days' time he would be far less willing to come into the cathedral; and yet perhaps he, as head of the town council, should do the great, the noble thing; perhaps he should enter the finished cathedral first. He shivered. He was not a hero, and had no desire to be one. Should he volunteer his own soul at this afternoon's council meeting? He did not want to. He was afraid.

He knelt down before the altar and prayed to God to help him.

Suddenly he was distracted by a light step behind him. He turned his head and saw a young friar looking down at him.

"I think I may be able to help you," said the friar.

THE LAST detail of the last carving was chiselled. The last glass was in its place. The workmen scurried away from the cathedral, anxious in case the last soul to leave should be mistaken for the first soul to enter the finished building. There was only one thing left to do; the great West door that the Devil himself had undertaken to make was not yet hanging in the huge main porchway. The whole town waited in suspense.

He came with a curious growl. It was a sound the people had never heard before, but nobody doubted that it came from the Devil. It started softly, then grew louder and louder until it throbbed in the ears of every inhabitant of Aix. Only a few people saw him, and then for less than a second. For he no longer looked like a magnificent high-ranking gentleman. Now the sight of him was intolerable to the human eye. Those who saw him turned away in agony and despair.

The heavy door thudded into place on its hinges. Satan admired his handiwork for a moment; even God should be impressed by those bronze lions, he thought. Then he pulled the door open, and waited quietly and patiently, hidden behind it.

One by one, people crept out of their houses and hiding-places. They no longer heard the throbbing growl; the frightful vision was gone. Only the new door, standing open, told them of the Devil's presence. Nobody approached it. But Satan did not mind. The Mayor and town councillors had pledged him a soul. They had no alternative but to keep their promise.

Then the people, who had been staring fixedly at the door, began to turn their heads. A procession was slowly coming towards the cathedral—the councillors of Aix, led by the Mayor. They were carrying a huge box, made out of thick slats of wood, through which a dark shape could be seen moving. Behind them walked a young friar.

A buzz of excitement and anguish filled the air. A terrible

event was about to take place. The people were going to witness not just death but damnation. The Devil rejoiced silently at his success.

The procession stopped in front of the open door. Solemnly the councillors lowered their burden to the ground. Townspeople and Devil studied their faces, searching for the terror that would reveal to them who was to be Satan's victim.

The friar crossed himself. Then he nodded to the Mayor. The Devil prepared to pounce. Some spectators screamed, others turned away; some fainted, others prayed. The Mayor stepped forward fearlessly.

But he did not go through the great West door of the cathedral. Instead he tore three slats of wood from the front of the box. At the same moment the councillors began hammering on it, yelling at the tops of their voices. Out through the open slats and into the cathedral shot—a wolf. The Devil pounced, claiming the first soul to enter the finished building.

Too late he realized what he had done. He had taken a soul that was of no use to him—the soul of an animal. With an angry howl, he hurled himself out of the great door, banging it savagely behind him. The howl became wild with pain and fury. He had caught his hand in the door. He tried to wrench it away. But his thumb was stuck fast. Half-crazy with misery and humiliation, he gave one last stupendous tug. He was free. But the thumb was not. It remained caught for ever, in the mouth of a bronze lion. It is still there today.

THE MAYOR stood in the cathedral—a magnificent monument to the glory of God and Emperor Charles the Great, and the pride and joy of the City of Aix. In his hand he was holding the document that the young friar had studied so carefully for him: "We, the Mayor and Councillors of that same town, do promise Satan the first soul that enters . . ."

Poor devil, thought the Mayor, fancy his leaving out the word *human*. He shuddered; but for the Devil's carelessness and the friar's cleverness, that soul might well have been his.

As it was, he had triumphed. All the citizens of Aix were congratulating him. Even the councillors were congratulating him. Soon the Emperor would also congratulate him. He crushed the document in his hand, just as a victorious mayor might crush a devil.

10

An Unholy Friar: the Story of Doctor Faustus and Mephistophilis

"I'M BORED, bored, bored!" shouted the Doctor, slamming the book shut on his desk. He stared thoughtfully into the fire. Then he got up, picked up the book, and tossed it into the flames. The fire went dull, filling the study with smoke.

"Damnation," muttered the Doctor under his breath. The smoke was getting thicker and heavier. He began to cough. He opened the door and yelled:

"Wagner!"

Christoph Wagner came scurrying down the passageway, to be met by a great cloud of smoke. Dimly he could see his master standing in the doorway.

"The fire needs attention," said Doctor Faustus.

"Seems to have come out looking for it, sir," replied Christoph chirpily. The doctor did not seem to be amused, so Christoph hurried across to see to the fire. Funny that it should be smoking like that; he had put nothing but dry wood on it. Then, through the smoke, he saw the book. Really, his master was impossible sometimes! That wouldn't do book or fire any good at all! Carefully Christoph extracted the book with the tongs. Immediately the fire flared up again. He examined the book to see the extent of the damage; what he saw made him cry out in horror.

"Sir! You put the Holy Bible on the fire!"

Johannes Faustus was a Doctor of Divinity at the University of Wittenberg in Germany. He found Divinity an easy but dull subject. He was expected to learn all sorts of facts about religion, without ever questioning their truth. That was not done in 1520. But Faustus had a scientific mind. Other subjects had more to offer: mathematics, medicine, and astrology—the study of the stars and their influences on human life, a subject that many of his contemporaries considered dangerous and evil. And now he had discovered a new science that fascinated him more than any other—black magic. Here, he felt, was the way to know, experience, understand and enjoy more, to make his life more worthwhile. The Holy Bible offered no such prospect. It was useless. So he threw it on the fire.

He was not pleased when Christoph put it back in his hands.

"If it won't burn, go and bury it!" he snapped.

"B-but . . ." stammered Christoph, appalled at the sacreligious task.

"Do as you're told!" shouted Faustus.

Christoph scuttled away. As soon as he was gone the Doctor took another thick book from his shelf. This time it was a book of black magic. He put on his cloak and went out of the house, hiding the book under his arm.

Dusk was gathering. Faustus turned in the direction of the wood that lay a little way out of the town. As he walked, his gloomy irritation began to lift. He felt sorry that he had been bad-tempered with Christoph. The little servant could not be expected to understand that the Doctor of Divinity had found a new religion. Faustus walked with an eager step now. He was going to conjure up the Devil.

At the centre of the wood was a small clearing. There Faustus drew a large circle in the dusty earth. Within it he drew weird signs that he copied to the last detail from the book he was holding. Around the edge, he wrote in satanic script—backwards and in mirror fashion—the Lord's Prayer. The tall fir trees around him made the evening dark. Faustus knew that the moment had almost come. He stood at the centre of the circle, waiting.

He did not intend to summon Lucifer, chief of all devils. His studies had led him to believe that Lucifer would be too powerful for him, and might even destroy him. He wanted a devil he could control, who would be his servant, his helper, his friend, not his master. He wanted:

"MEPHISTOPHILIS!"

He roared the devil's name into the night.

For a second the forest was uncannily still. Then suddenly it was possessed by violent life. A deafening howl filled the trees, which bent sideways as if contorted by a hurricane. Faustus covered his ears with his hands, trying to block out the din ripping at his eardrums. But nothing dulled the agonizing sound. Instead, above it, he heard a pounding and drumming like giant hooves. Then he saw flames everywhere, all around him, curling, licking, grabbing at the night. It was no good. He could not stay and face this terrible devil that he had summoned. The only thing Faustus wanted

to do now was to step out of his conjuring circle and hurry back home to find his Bible.

No sooner had this thought crossed his mind than the noise and the flames subsided, and instead Faustus heard music, more beautiful and more alluring than anything he had heard before. Visions of women with long, golden, mermaid hair, of glittering wines, of gold coins pouring from jewelled chests cloaked his senses. The wish to leave the enchanted circle vanished. Faustus felt brave and strong now. Thrilled and marvelling, he called again:

"MEPHISTOPHILIS!"

A second howl drowned the music, a howl of monstrous mocking laughter; coming from directly above Faustus's head. The sky was bright with flames that were moving slowly together to form a huge fiery globe. Suddenly the mocking howl ceased, and, with a high-pitched wail, the globe began to spin around Faustus's head, coming closer and closer.

This devil was making fun of him. Half terrified, half furious, Faustus cried out a third time,

"MEPHISTOPHILIS!"

Slowly the globe began to shrink, and then to change its shape, until with a hiss the flames vanished, and Faustus saw before him an ordinary friar, with a little bald tonsure in the middle of his head, and dressed in a long brown robe.

"Mephistophilis at your service," said the friar, with a polite little bow.

Now that he had settled on a human shape, Mephistophilis seemed everything that Faustus could wish for in a devil. They walked back together through the forest to Faustus's house, and Mephistophilis listened most attentively while Faustus explained about the dissatisfaction he felt with his studies in Divinity and with everything life had offered him so far. Mephistophilis answered that he was quite sure he would be able to help. He was willing to teach, serve, provide unlimited money, and see to it that Faustus had more excitement and enjoyment than any man had ever known. Moreover, he would be very happy to stay with Faustus for the next twenty-four years. As payment, he required very little, and he would not be asking for that until the twenty-four years were up. He wanted only Faustus's soul.

Even so, Faustus had his doubts.

"How long will you keep my soul?" he asked.

"For ever," replied the devil with a smile.

"For ever" sounds a very long time. But you cannot pin it down and imagine it as you can with a precise time, like twenty-four years, which also sounds very long. Besides, that "for ever" would not even begin for twenty-four years, and those twenty-four years would be wonderful, and they could begin now, as soon as Faustus agreed to part with his soul. Somehow, the twenty-four years seemed longer and more important to Faustus than "for ever".

"Where will you keep my soul?"

"In Hell, of course," answered Mephistophilis.

Why should Faustus be afraid of Hell anyway? He did not believe what the Bible and the Church said about all those torments. Mephistophilis came from there, and *he* seemed cheerful enough. Why give up a glorious life for some shadow of misery that might not even exist?

"I agree," said Faustus, and held out his hand to the friar.

But Mephistophilis did not take his hand.

"I need your signature," he said, producing a document from the folds of his habit. Faustus glanced at it. It was written in mirror fashion, but Faustus had studied black magic enough to read it easily.

"Mephistophilis promises to serve Johannes Faustus, body and soul, for twenty-four years, and to fulfil his every desire. In return, I, Johannes Faustus, swear that I will always deny and oppose the Christian faith, and, when the time is up, will give myself, body and soul, to Lucifer."

"Fine!" said Faustus. He led his new friend into his study, took a quill and dipped it into the inkstand. He was about to sign when Mephistophilis laid his hand gently on his wrist, indicating the vein.

"In blood," said the devil, handing him a sharp narrow blade. Faustus felt suddenly less bold; but he gingerly cut the small vein leading to his left palm. Blood gushed out of the wound. Faustus held his hand so that the blood should collect in a pool at the centre of the palm.

But the blod did not flow normally. It grew thick, forming shapes! Letters! Words! Faustus could read them now.

"TAKE FLIGHT FAUSTUS."

Faustus stared in horror. Then he turned to Mephistophilis. In vain! The figure of the friar was fading before his eyes. A moment later it was gone.

Where did those words come from? Was it God, warning him not to sign the Devil's document? Faustus gazed at the sinister command, congealed and red on his hand. Tremblingly he put down his quill.

A moment later he snatched it up again. Was he going to let three words change his mind? Was it worse to be the Devil's slave than God's slave? At least the Devil had promised twenty-four good years.

Faustus took a small saucer. He held his hand over the flames of the fire so that the words slowly dissolved and the blood dripped down into the saucer. Then he dipped the quill into the red pool and signed the document. Immediately it was snatched from his hand. The friar was back.

A YEAR had gone by. Christoph Wagner was setting out the gold plates on the delicately carved table. This certainly wasn't like the old days, thought Christoph. Where his master got such expensive things from he could not think. But he wasn't bothered. If his master lived like a king, he lived like a king's servant.

The only thing that did bother him was that friar. You never knew whether he was coming or going. Christoph would be quietly helping himself from a flagon of his master's wine, thinking he was all alone, when he would turn round and find the friar standing right beside him. Not that the friar ever said anything. It was just the way he grinned, almost greedily—quite an unholy look for a friar.

Just then there was a knock on the door. It was his master's supper guest—a very clever and serious divinity student called Martin. He looked, Christoph thought, even more strained and anxious than usual. Instead of going straight to join the Doctor in his study, Martin grasped Christoph by the arm and tugged him away to the far end of the corridor.

"I'm terribly worried about the Doctor!" he whispered urgently.

Christoph stared at Martin amazed. He would do better to worry about himself, behaving in this peculiar manner. His master had never been so happy and prosperous as now.

"Every time I have attended his lectures this year, I have heard him preach against God and Jesus Christ. I am afraid he may have come under an evil influence." Martin blurted out the fear that had been haunting him for months.

Christoph could not stop himself from laughing.

"If that's all you're worried about, you can set your mind at rest," he said. "He's had a holy friar living in this very house for this past year."

Martin was surprised. He had never seen the friar. Nevertheless he felt very relieved. He loved and admired the Doctor. He did not want to see him come to any harm. He smiled at Christoph gratefully.

The smile encouraged Christoph to tell a little more.

"Mind you," he said, "there was a time when I was worried too, the night before the friar came here, in fact. My master made me bury the Holy Bible that night."

Martin turned pale. Christoph was pleased to be having such an effect and went on to tell the whole story, including how, later on, his master had insisted on him burying all the rest of his divinity books.

"But what about the friar?" stuttered Martin. "Did he not want you to dig them up again?"

"Oh no! He brought other books instead," Christoph replied, "but I couldn't read them. They were all back to front."

Martin felt hot, then cold. He grabbed the astonished servant by the shoulders and shook him violently.

"Do you realize what you are saying?" Martin shouted at him. "Those books you couldn't read were books of black magic, infernal books! The friar who brought them into the house is not a holy friar! Your master is under an evil influence! The friar is evil!"

Christoph remembered the friar's grin on seeing him pilfer wine. Unholy. Martin's words did make sense.

"So that's where all the money comes from!" he exclaimed. "He's got a devil for a servant!... I hope he doesn't turn me out," he added, looking perturbed.

"He could do much worse than that," said Martin passionately. "He could give the Devil his immortal soul."

Christoph was not so sure that that would be worse, but he agreed with Martin that it would not be good, and that somebody should give his master a good talking-to, as long as he himself did not have to do it.

Martin spoke to Faustus that same evening, when they were alone together before supper—a supper that poor Martin never had a chance to eat. He begged him from the bottom of his heart to send away his dreadful companion.

Although he had felt nervous about it, Martin was not ready for what the Doctor did. His face went white; his whole body stiffened. Then he hurled himself upon the unlucky student and gripped his neck in both hands. Martin began to choke; he struggled frantically to escape the throttling hands, then fell down limply at the Doctor's feet.

Christoph came running when he heard the struggle. He saw Martin lying on the floor and his master standing over him with murder in his eyes. His master was unsheathing a knife.

"No, sir." he shrieked, rushing across the room towards him.

To his astonishment the Doctor dropped the knife.

"All right," he said casually, "just throw him out." Then he sat down at the supper table as if nothing had happened.

Wondering at his master's cruelty, Christoph bent down over Martin, who was moaning weakly. Gently he helped him to his feet.

"Let me take him out for you." Christoph started at the sudden voice in his ear. It was the friar.

The friar helped Martin courteously to the door, apologizing humbly for the doctor's bad manners. Just before he left the student staggering on the street outside he asked if he could give a word of advice.

"Don't waste your time on the Doctor. It could be extremely dangerous." Then he added with a conspiratorial wink, "Besides, he has me to take care of him."

Martin was found lying in the street on the following day. He was ill for several months. When at last he was well enough to go on with his studies, he followed the devil's advice and kept away from Doctor Faustus.

THE DOCTOR settled down to his supper with relish. Mephistophilis had brought him a dish of exotic sea fruits from the coast of Africa. They were delicious. Faustus sipped a glass of golden wine, spirited away from the Bishop of Saltzburg's cellar. This was the life! Forget Martin!

But Martin was beginning to bother Faustus. What had possessed him to attack the student? He had never done anything like that before. Some madness must have taken him over. He might have killed the boy, who was after all only speaking out of genuine concern. Then a second worry started. Perhaps Martin was right, and he should send Mephistophilis away.

Perhaps there was still time to repent.

Faustus put down his fork and went upstairs to his bedroom, shutting the door carefully so that Mephistophilis should not disturb him. Then he knelt down beside his bed. But no sooner had he done so than Mephistophilis was there in front of him, hissing angrily, his friar's features changing into an ugly grimace. Faustus shuddered with a sudden chill. Yet why should he let this monster rule his life—and his death?

"Lord God, please help me," he prayed for the first time in many years.

Almost as soon as he had uttered the words, Mephistophilis began to fade and blur before him. Then he was gone. Faustus stood up with a light heart. It had been so easy. He would go and apologize to Martin tomorrow, and return to his old life.

He would have done better to have stayed on his knees.

Thick, hot, stinking yellow smoke was engulfing him. A bitter cold was eating into his body. A deafening roar filled the air.

"If you repent, Lucifer will tear you in a thousand pieces!"

A ghastly shape loomed before him in the smoke. Its body was the colour of dried blood, and covered in hairs that writhed like tiny snakes. Its thick, forked tail lashed from side to side. It must be Lucifer himself. Faustus shrank away as the Devil lowered over him, gnashing its black fangs. Many shapes were forming in the smoke now, a devil with wings of fire and a bull's head from which long ears trailed on the ground; a dragon devil, covered with spines like daggers; a devil with the head of an ass; devils like dogs, hogs, toads, cats, serpents—stinking, screeching, lurching nearer and nearer towards Faustus. If this was what repentance brought, Faustus wanted nothing more of it.

"Stop! I curse God! I curse Jesus Christ! I curse the Holy Ghost!"

In a flash smoke and devils vanished. Only the friar stood

beside him. "Mephistophilis at your service," he said with a polite bow again.

It was several years before Faustus was tempted to try and escape the Devil again. Mephistophilis worked very hard to make sure that he had no wish to. They were marvellous years. Faustus ate and drank better than any king. He had exquisite clothes that he never wore more than once. He was constantly surrounded by beautiful women. He travelled throughout the universe with his devil, spinning through time and space in a great golden globe, dazzled by the brilliance of stars and moons and with the excitement of discovery. He felt for himself the glow of the fiery stars and the cool damp of the clouds. He saw for himself that the earth revolved round the sun and, when he returned from his travels, he stunned the world with these revelations. He became famous for his scientific knowledge. No glory, no pleasure was denied him. He revelled in his life.

And then he met the girl.

He passed her in the streets of Wittenberg one day when he was on his way to give a lecture at the University. He smiled at her, liking her gentle eyes. She smiled back shyly. There was something about her that made Faustus feel warm and cheerful. He felt he wanted to be friends with her. He suddenly realized that he no longer had any friends and, in spite of his wonderful adventures, that he was very lonely. He slowed down, intending to speak to her. Her smile became more confident. She seemed to like him too. Faustus felt extraordinarily happy.

Suddenly her expression changed. She turned away from Faustus and ran off down the street. Faustus heard a soft laugh close to his ear. It was the friar.

"Where did you spring from?" shouted Faustus angrily.

"She didn't seem to like me," grinned Mephistophilis.

"Then stay away from her!"

"I was going to suggest you did the same."

Faustus took no notice. The devil's intervention only made him more determined to follow the flaxen-haired girl. How dare he try and tell him what to do! He was meant to *grant* Faustus's wishes, not thwart them. He could just see the girl, a small dot in the distance. He set off at a run after her, but she would not stop. She was running as though her soul depended on it. Faustus chased her blindly. Soon he had almost caught up. He followed her into what seemed to be a huge porch.

Then a searing pain caught him in the side, taking his breath away. His head began to spin. He could go no farther. The girl disappeared through the door.

He heard music and singing. It was then that he realized he was in the porchway of a church. She must be in the church itself by now. He staggered forward, determined not to let her go. Immediately pains like red-hot pincers took hold of his whole body. Unable to bear them, he stumbled backwards away from the church. The pains stopped. Sadly he made his way home.

"You made a real fool of yourself this time," said the friar, who was sitting comfortably in the Doctor's chair.

"Don't you mean you made a fool of me?" retorted Faustus. "Our agreement states that you are to serve me, not get in my way."

"Our agreement also says that you are to deny and oppose the Christian faith, body and soul, and yet you allowed that girl to lead you into church."

"That was because I want her!" replied Faustus. "And I demand to see her again!"

"But she is repulsively pure and loves God. She doesn't like evil things. You saw how she ran away from me. She wouldn't want anything to do with you."

"If I saw her again, I would make her love me—"

"You'll be wanting to get married next," interrupted the devil.

"Why not?"

Mephistophilis stood up. His face widened into an evil grin. Then he began to laugh. The laugh grew louder and louder. Scales covered his body. His hands took the form of great claws. He towered over Faustus, laughing.

"Fool! Marriage belongs to God. Love belongs to God. The girl belongs to God. You belong to the Devil. You cannot escape. There is no escape!" The huge claws bore down on Faustus. At the same time, he felt the tearing pains again, all over his body. The devil's laughter thundered in his ears. It was intolerable.

"Let go of me, please," screamed Faustus. "I'll forget all about her! I swear!"

"Excellent!" said the friar, sitting down again.

FAUSTUS DID NOT forget the girl quite as easily as Mephistophilis wished. He tried to shut her out of his mind, but the memory of her face would surge up, filling him with regret at having lost her. But with the devil's help he could always blot out the memory and conquer the regret. He drank wine so strong that it turned the world into a glorious dream, where brilliant images dazzled his mind, where the air was gentle and warm, and where the only sounds were music. Or he would fly through the real world with Mephistophilis, meeting kings of every land, eating their choicest food, stealing their best wine and seducing their prettiest wives, learning everything there was to know, and seeing everything there was to see. Then he had to admit that Mephistophilis was right about the girl. Love and marriage were not for him. They would have ruined his life.

As the years went by, Faustus chased pleasure and excitement more and more frantically. For the time when he would have to pay for it all was approaching. He was determined to have no regrets.

Yet his doubts were still growing. He had everything, had done everything, but he was still not quite satisfied. He still wished for something; but there was nothing left to wish for. It was almost worse than if he had never had the chance to be rich and learned and to enjoy himself so much. He could no longer blot out the vision of the flaxen-haired girl. It seemed to Faustus that she was the only thing he had ever wanted—the one thing that Mephistophilis had denied him. He began to accuse the devil of not keeping his side of the bargain they had made. Mysterious pains again attacked Faustus, but they no longer silenced him. The devil had to try something else.

"If I brought the most beautiful woman that ever existed to live with you till the end of your life, would you be satisfied then?" he asked Faustus wearily.

Again the vision of the girl surged into Faustus's mind. He shook his head. But as he did so he saw the image of a different woman, dark-haired and far, far more beautiful.

"Is that her?" he gasped.

The devil nodded.

"She is Helen of Troy," he said. "The Trojans fought the Greeks for her. Now she can be yours." He glanced at Faustus slyly. "If you want her."

"I do," whispered Faustus, destroying for ever his memory of the flaxen-haired girl. Immediately Helen stood at his side. Doubts and pains vanished.

FAUSTUS AND HELEN had a child, a little boy, as beautiful as his mother and as intelligent as his father. Faustus was proud to possess Helen; but he loved the boy. He spent hours playing with him and teaching him. He was sure now that he had not wasted his soul. For after his death his son would inherit all his wealth and learning. Any suffering would be worth while because the boy would carry on living for him.

Christoph noticed a change in his master. He was happier and more gentle than before. He no longer had so much time for that devil of a friar. Perhaps the Doctor would save himself after all.

But this hope was short-lived.

One night when he went into his master's study to lay the fire, Christoph found Faustus doubled up in his chair clutching his arms against his stomach; tears of pain were trickling down his ashen face.

"Sir, what is the matter?"

Faustus smiled grimly. "Nothing you or I can put right," he said. A second pain swept through his body, making him cry out sharply.

Christoph felt suddenly afraid for his master. Perhaps he was dying.

"Shall I fetch a physician, sir?" he said. "Or a priest?"

"There is no need. I am here," said another voice. As usual the friar had appeared out of nowhere. Christoph saw his master shudder. A grim shadow of death seemed to pass over him. Christoph took a step towards Faustus, wanting to protect him from the evil friar. But the crisis seemed to be over. Faustus sat up straight.

"You can go to bed now, Wagner," he said.

However, Christoph worried more and more about his master. Every day the Doctor's face looked a little more strained and grey, as if some terrible disease was eating at him from within. Christoph often heard him raving and crying out at night. He was quite sure Faustus was getting no sleep at all. He drank strong liquor all the time, but not for pleasure now, only to deaden his pain. The only thing that seemed to lighten his distress was the little boy. Faustus played with him as long as he had the strength.

At last Christoph could bear it no longer. He had to try and find help for his master, whatever that friar might think about it.

There was only one person to whom he could turn. Martin was now himself a distinguished Doctor of Divinity, who had taken Faustus's place teaching at the University. Martin had not seen Faustus since the night Mephistophilis had left him staggering at the door twenty-three years ago, but he had kept in touch with Christoph and had never ceased to show concern for his former teacher.

"My master is very sick," blurted out Christoph as soon as he was shown into Martin's study. Martin's hair was grey now. He looked even more strained and serious than he had as a student. He took the news calmly. He had expected it.

"Please," went on Christoph, "can you help him?"

The servant was desperate. But Martin did not see what he could do.

"I have already failed to help him," he said.

"That was a long time ago. He needs help now," pleaded Christoph.

"He did then, too."

"But he didn't know it then. He knows now."

Martin looked gravely at Christoph's anxious face. Am I afraid that the sick old Doctor will try to kill me again? he asked himself. Am I afraid to fight the Devil? If Faustus is on my side, might I not yet win?

"I'll come and see him," he said. The hours in between he spent in prayer.

Faustus welcomed Martin friendlily. He seemed pleased to see him. He looked very ill, but tried to be cheerful and hospitable.

"I'm glad to have some company this evening," he said.

Martin noticed that the friar was not there. "Where's your . . ." he hesitated.

"My devil?" laughed Faustus drily. "I sent him away. He's getting on my nerves at the moment." Faustus shuddered. For a moment he seemed to forget all about Martin. He glanced at the clock. Martin noticed that it was just a little past six. He did not know that Faustus had less than six hours to live. The Doctor looked back at Martin, pleading. He was terrified to be alone.

"I still owe you a supper. Will you stay and have supper with me?" Martin nodded.

The Doctor went on, chatting nervously; "I did try to take your advice, you know, that night I nearly throttled you."

This was Martin's cue. He must speak.

"Try again now!"

"It's too late." The Doctor's voice sounded flat and hopeless. He had stopped pretending. He was as good as dead.

But Martin was ready to fight.

"It's never too late! If you really try! If God knows you are deeply repentant!"

A spark of hope glimmered in Faustus's deadened eyes. "Do you really believe that?" he asked.

"Yes! Can you still pray?"

"I should like to try."

For a moment Martin thought that Faustus was going down on his knees to God. But Faustus was not kneeling; he was crouching, doubled up, clutching both sides, his face distorted with pain.

"It's too late," he said for the second time, breathless in the vicious grip of the pain. Immediately the agony was over. His face relaxed. He stood up.

"Let us eat," he said. His face was appallingly grey.

Martin wondered what to do next. The Devil certainly had tremendous power over Faustus. He knew that he could not take on the Devil alone if he did not have a weapon to use against him. Suddenly he turned to Christoph.

"Please bring me a Bible."

"No!" The Doctor's voice rang out in panic. He could not stand any more pain. "I have only three more hours to live! Don't take them away! If you bring the Bible I will be torn to pieces!"

Martin and Christoph stared in horror. Neither of them had suspected that Faustus's end was so near. They had very little time.

"And if we don't bring the Bible?" Martin asked urgently.

"I will still be torn to pieces, but not yet!" Anything to put off the pain and stay alive for three more hours! thought Faustus in despair.

"And your Immortal soul?"

"It will go to Hell." Faustus spoke up bravely, but his voice trembled with fear.

"But you cannot allow that to happen," insisted Martin. "You must let us help you. We can save your soul."

"And what about my body?" asked Faustus wryly.

Martin shook his head. "It is too late to save that."

"But my body is more afraid than my soul!" cried Faustus. "I must go on living as long as I can!"

"So just for three more hours of life, you will not try to escape Hell?"

"No!"

It was hopeless. No one could save Faustus if he did not want to be saved. Martin rose from his seat.

"I am going. I am no use here."

Faustus clutched his arm like a drowning man grasping at a board. "Please stay! I have a favour to ask you."

Martin looked down at the hollow, fear-stricken eyes. The least he could do was to try to comfort Faustus before his plunge into endless pain and darkness. He sat down again.

They sat there silently with their eyes on the clock, as one, then two, hours passed. Christoph, standing behind them, shifted uneasily from foot to foot.

Suddenly Faustus stood up.

"Let me show you my son." He led Martin along a corridor to a little room where the little boy lay sleeping peacefully. He stood for a moment, admiring him for the last time.

"He will be my heir," he said. Will you take care of him and teach him for me?"

"I shall care for him as if he were my own son," said Martin, taking Faustus by the hand.

Thankful for this last strand of comfort, Faustus turned towards the bedroom door. Beyond it was pain and terror.

"Stay with him now," he said, and vanished into the dark corridor.

Martin sat down beside the boy. He heard a clock strike—half past eleven, a quarter to twelve, midnight. He thought he heard a cry in the distance. He ran to the door; then turned back, remembering the child for whom he was now responsible. The bed was empty, as if it had never been slept in. So even the boy had been one of the Devil's tricks to damn the Doctor. Martin shook his head sadly, wondering what had driven a man like Faustus to such wickedness.

Christoph, listening nervously as he cleared the supper table, also heard the cry. It came from his master's study. He raced along the corridor and flung open the door. Doctor Faustus lay dead on the polished floor. A little pool of blood was trickling from his mouth. The servant's eyes filled with tears.

"Cheer up!"

Christoph turned and saw the friar. He was holding out a book to Christoph. "You might find this useful," he said.

Without thinking, Christoph took the book and opened it. It was written mirror-fashion. Christoph gave a cry of terror and flung the book on to the fire, then turned angrily on the devil who had brought about his master's misery. But the friar was fading into the night air. A moment later he was gone. The fire hissed and crackled, then burst into bright flames, devouring the book of black magic.